ATTITUDES THROUGH IDIOMS

Thomas W. Adams
University of Petroleum and Minerals
Dhahran, Saudi Arabia

Susan R. Kuder
Cross-Cultural Specialist
Boston, Massachusetts

HEINLE & HEINLE PUBLISHERS
A Division of Wadsworth, Inc.
Boston, Massachusetts 02116

Library of Congress Cataloging in Publication Data

Adams, Thomas W., 1951—
    Attitudes through idioms.

    1. English language--Text-books for foreign
speakers.   2. English language--Idioms.   I. Kuder,
Susan R., 1943–   II. Title.
Pe1128.A299   1984   428.1   83-17209
ISBN 0-8384-2650-6

Illustrations by Peter Zafris

Cover and text design by Diana Esterly

First printing: February 1984

Printed in the U.S.A.

63-20030

13 14

Notes to the Instructor

PURPOSE AND APPROACH OF THE BOOK

The dual purpose of this book is to teach idioms used in the United States and to provide insight into North American cultural attitudes. The book is made up of units that are organized around an attitude and that introduce idioms illustrating that attitude.

LEVEL OF THE BOOK

Attitudes through Idioms is appropriate for intermediate to advanced students. All lessons are of approximately the same level of difficulty. Discrete by nature, they need not be assigned sequentially.

FORMAT AND PROCEDURE

Each lesson is composed of six parts: *Situation, Analysis, Explanation, Attitude, Expansion,* and *Communication.* An answer key and a glossary are in the back of the book.

Situation, Analysis, and *Explanation:* Idioms that express the attitude being dealt with are introduced in a conversational setting (*Situation*). The conversation is then followed by a question that relates to the meaning of the idioms and the attitude they reflect (*Analysis*). Three choices are provided as possible answers to the question. Once students choose an answer, they can verify their choice by turning the page (*Explanation*).

Attitude: The attitude being treated is stated in the form of an opinion of one or more of the characters in the *Situation.* Students may agree or disagree based on their own experiences; they may talk about whether this attitude is valued in their own countries; they may talk about whether they feel the attitude is a thing to be valued.

Expansion: Additional idioms that relate to the attitude are introduced in an exercise format. Answers to the first two exercises A and B are in the Answer Key at the back of the book.

Communication: Questions in this part of the lesson provide communicative practice in using the idioms and in further discussing the target attitude.

INSTRUCTIONS ON USE

The text is highly flexible, allowing instructors to spend as much or as little class time on the lessons as they see fit. Lessons can be done individually, in small groups, or as a class. An intermediate student working alone can do the first five components (*Situation, Analysis, Explanation, Attitude,* and *Expansion*) in about thirty minutes. Working with others and discussing the lesson together would take a bit longer. The *Communication* questions generally require more extensive thought, and can be prepared as written assignments or as in-class discussion topics.

Acknowledgments

The authors wish to acknowledge the valuable comments and suggestions made by students at Harvard University Summer School who were enrolled in the course, "Inside American Culture through Idioms."

Contents

1
Perseverance

give up
go through with something
hang in there

stick with something
sweat something out

SITUATION Read the following dialog:

Sue is taking a statistics course, which she finds very difficult. She is talking about the course with her roommate, Chris.

Sue: Chris, I'm thinking about dropping my statistics course. I've been sitting here for an hour working on the same problem and I can't solve it.

Chris: I know how you feel. I had that class last semester and wanted to drop it after the first day, but I decided to **stick with** it and I'm glad I did. By the time it was over, I had really learned a lot.

Sue: Yeah, I suppose I shouldn't **give up** just because it's hard.

Chris: If you drop it, you'll disappoint yourself. In the end, you'll be glad you took it.

ANALYSIS Circle the best answer to the question below. Then turn the page and read the explanation for your choice. If you are wrong, choose again.

Why does Chris think that it is better for Sue not to drop her statistics course?

A. She thinks that because Sue decided to take the course, she should complete it.

B. She thinks that because Sue finds math easy, she will do well in the course, even though she does not like it.

C. If Sue continues with the course, Chris will help her study and Sue will pass.

1

EXPLANATION A. Chris thinks that because Sue started the course, she should finish it, even if it is difficult. She convinces Sue of this when she tells her about her own experience with the course. This is the best answer.

B. Sue said that the course was difficult, not easy, and is afraid that she will not do well.

C. It is true that because Sue and Chris appear to be good friends, Chris might help Sue, but there is nothing in the conversation that says so.

ATTITUDE **Chris feels that when people start something, however difficult, they should continue with it, if it is in their best interest to do so.**

EXPANSION A. Put a checkmark (✓) if the person continues with something already started.

✓   Karen is part of a study group that meets once a week in the library. However, she has been very busy lately and has been thinking of leaving the group. After some thought, however, she decides to **stick with** it. She puts on her coat, gathers her books, and goes to the library.

_____ 1. Brian is very nervous about marrying Ann. One day he wants to do it, and the next he does not. On the day of the wedding, he decides to **go through with** it. He puts on his best clothes and goes to church.

_____ 2. John is trying to repair his television set. He has no idea what is wrong with it and he is ready to **give up** and call in a professional to repair his set. He goes to the phone.

_____ 3. Margaret is at a party where she does not know anyone and all the people she has met are boring. She wants to leave, but she does not want to offend the host. She decides to **sweat it out**. She sits down and starts talking to someone.

_____ 4. Fred signed up for four years in the army, but is thinking about leaving after two. He has a nice job waiting for him in the family business. In the end, however, he decides to **hang in there** and not leave because he feels he should honor his contract. He writes a letter to his family to tell them of his decision.

B. In each of the following, there is a sentence that does not fit. Find it and cross it out.

Sally usually **sticks with** something to the end. She feels that if she starts something, she should finish it. ~~Once she read half a book and then returned it to the library~~. Another time, she spent a whole day completing a crossword puzzle.

1. Laura is taking a college entrance exam, but she does not feel well. She is going to try to **sweat it out** and finish the test even though she still has an hour to go. She puts on her coat to leave. Then she goes to the next question and answers it.

2. Bill is someone who **hangs in there**. He decided to build his own house and had all sorts of problems. The boards were not cut properly, the pipes were too small, and the glass kept breaking. But did Bill stop? Yes, he did. He and his family moved into their new house six months later.

3. George always **gives up**. He never tries. He does not finish anything that he starts. He is not someone you would want to work with. I do not see how he will ever succeed in this world. George would make a good leader.

4. Richard has agreed to go to a party with his wife, but now he says he would rather just stay at home. His wife, however, wants him to go and thinks that Richard should ***go through with*** it. She told him that if he does not want to go, he should not. She said he should not have accepted the invitation if he did not plan to attend.

C. Complete the following sentences with the appropriate idiomatic expression. Make sure it fits the blanks.

give up   *stick with it*
go through with   *sweat it out*
hang in there

Karen entered a dance contest. After two hours, her feet hurt so much that she had to _give_ _up_ .

1. Amy started a new job which she finds very difficult. She is tempted to quit, but her boss tells her it is always hard in the beginning and it will get easier as time goes on. Amy has confidence in her boss and decides to _____ ____ in _____ .

2. Mike took a final examination in history and did not think that he did well. He wanted to know right away if he passed or not, but the teacher was slow in correcting the exams. Mike just had to _____ it _____ .

3. Although Greg did not enjoy his summer job as a construction worker, he decided to _____ _____ it because the money was good.

4. Stewart and Gail had planned a hiking trip for the weekend. When they listened to the weather forecast, they heard that it might rain. They decided to ____ _____ with the trip anyway because it was the only weekend they had free.

COMMUNICATION   Read and discuss the following:

1. Think of a time when you had to choose between ***sweating it out*** or ***giving up***. What was it and why did you do what you did? Do you feel now that your decision was a good one? Why or why not?

2. You and your friends have decided to go mountain climbing. In the early morning, around eight o'clock, it is a beautiful day. By ten o'clock, the weather has changed, and it has started to rain. It would take two more hours to get to the top of the mountain. What would you decide to do—to ***stick with it*** and climb to the top, or to ***give up*** and turn back? Why?

3. Write a dialog like the one below that includes the expression **hang in there**.

   Stan and Jack are on the same track team. They are both long-distance runners.

   Stan: I'm beat. I don't think I can finish.

   Jack: We've only got two more miles to go.

   Stan: Every muscle in my body hurts.

   Jack: Come on. You can do it. **Hang in there**. Only a little bit farther.

   _____

   _____

   _____

   _____

   _____

   _____

4. When people **give up**, it might be because they see no chance of succeeding. However, if people want something badly enough, they usually can find a means to get it. This is the meaning of the proverb, "Where there's a will, there's a way." On a separate piece of paper, write a short story like the one below, based on this proverb.

   Benny's friend Barbara is in the hospital. It is Barbara's birthday, and Benny wants to see her. He gets to the hospital late because of traffic. It is after visiting hours and nobody will let him in. It is very important for Benny to see Barbara, so he dresses like a doctor and walks in the front door. Nobody stops him. Where there's a will, there's a way.

2
Responsibility

Leave someone

High and dry

duck the issue
face up to something
leave someone high and dry
pass the buck

point one's finger at someone
shoulder the responsibility
worm out of something

SITUATION Read the following dialog:

Ann Cooper, a doctor at the local hospital, agreed to organize a dinner honoring the hospital's volunteer workers. The following is a conversation with her husband, Harry.

Ann: Harry, I had no idea that organizing the dinner for volunteers was going to be so much work. I'm thinking of resigning.

Harry: Ann, you can't do that! You said that you would organize it, and now you have to **shoulder the responsibility**. You'll disappoint the hospital if you don't do what you said you would. When is the banquet, by the way?

Ann: Not until the middle of next month, but I've really got a busy schedule. I just don't see how I can get everything done.

Harry: But Ann, you know you're the best one for the job. That's why the hospital staff picked you to do it. They're depending on you, and if you resign, you'll **leave them high and dry**, with nobody to organize the dinner.

ANALYSIS Circle the best answer to the question below. Then turn the page and read the explanation for your choice. If you are wrong, choose again.

Why does Harry oppose Ann's resignation?

A. He knew his wife was a good cook and would prepare a good dinner.

B. He felt that because she said she would organize the banquet, she should do it.

C. He thought that his wife was exaggerating, and that organizing the banquet was not a lot of work.

EXPLANATION A. There is no reference to Mrs. Cooper's cooking in the conversation.

B. Mr. Cooper thought that because his wife had agreed to organize the banquet, she should take the responsibility for doing so. This is the best answer.

C. Mr. Cooper never commented on the amount of work his wife would have to do for the banquet.

ATTITUDE **Mr. Cooper feels that people should take responsibility for what they have committed themselves to do.**

EXPANSION A. Divide the following people into two groups. Group A is for those who accept responsibility and Group B is for those who do not.

Polly ***left us high and dry***. She agreed to be our treasurer, and then she suddenly resigned with nobody to replace her.

1. Pat always ***faces up to*** things. She never tries to avoid what is unpleasant.

2. Jack always ***passes the buck***. He always blames someone else when things go wrong.

3. Jill ***is ducking the issue*** under discussion. She is pretending she does not know what is being talked about.

4. Mary ***will shoulder the responsibility***. You can always depend on her.

5. Paul is trying to ***worm out of*** it. He said he would do it, and now he says he cannot because he has too many other things to do.

6. Mark always ***points his finger at*** someone else. He never takes the blame for anything he does.

Group A	Group B
	Polly

B. Put a plus sign (+) if you feel that the action reflects responsible behavior, and a minus sign (−) if you feel it does not.

____ The hospital in your hometown is running out of blood. A committee has been formed to organize a blood drive. On Saturday afternoon, volunteers will go to each house and ask the residents to donate blood. You agree to go to the houses on your street. Saturday morning, however, a friend asks you to go to a baseball game. You really want to see the game, so you go. You ***leave the committee high and dry***.

____ 1. You promised your little brother you would take him to the movies. A friend of yours calls, and asks you to a party. You want to go to the party, so you ***worm out of*** taking your brother to the movies.

_____ 2. Your boss tells you that your report is late. You are afraid of your boss, and **point your finger at** your secretary, saying that she was slow in typing it.

_____ 3. You have always been honest with your girlfriend. She wants to know where you were last night. You were out with another girl, and you do not want her to know it. When she asks, you **duck the issue**.

_____ 4. Your brother wants a new bike for his birthday. You want to buy him a bike, but you do not have enough money. For a while, you think about borrowing money from your father, but finally you **face up to** the fact that a bike is too expensive, and you buy him a baseball bat instead.

_____ 5. You and your sister are supposed to do the dishes before your parents return. Your sister goes to a movie with a friend. At 10:00 P.M. when your parents get home, the dishes are still not done. When your mother asks you why, you **pass the buck** and say it was your sister's fault.

_____ 6. Your English class wants to have a party. Your teacher agrees, and asks for someone to organize it. Although everybody wants a party, nobody volunteers. Finally, you **shoulder the responsibility** and agree to help your teacher organize it.

C. Mr. Tilson agreed to organize a picnic for the people he works with. Now he is sorry he agreed, and he wants to give the job to someone else. The reason is mainly because he feels that every time he makes a decision, Mr. Cotter, one of his co-workers, thinks it is a bad idea. Mr. Tilson's wife does not think he should quit. In fact, she thinks he is using Mr. Cotter as an excuse. Using the expressions below, write out what Mr. Tilson's wife says to him.

> **leave someone high and dry**   **worm out of something**
> **point one's finger at someone**   **shoulder the responsibility**
> **face up to something**

You said you would organize the picnic, and now you should shoulder the responsibility.

COMMUNICATION   Read and discuss the following:

1. Harry S. Truman, former President of the United States, had a sign on his desk that read, "The buck stops here." Using your knowledge of the expression ***pass the buck***, explain what Harry Truman meant.

2. People are sometimes blamed for something that they did not do. Children often ***point their finger at*** a brother or sister, claiming that he or she is the guilty one. Talk about a time when someone ***pointed his finger at*** you for something you were not responsible for.

3. Politicians are often accused of ***ducking the issues***, meaning that they avoid clearly stating their position. Why would someone who is running for office try to ***duck the issues***? Would you vote for a candidate who did this?

4. In all countries the government ***shoulders the responsibility*** for mail delivery and defense. What are some other things that governments ***shoulder the responsibility*** for?

3
Ease of Effort

Have A Green Thumb

be a breeze   have a green thumb
be all thumbs   have a knack for something
be easy as pie   have a nose for something
have a golden touch   have two left feet

SITUATION   Read the following dialog:

Mrs. Smith has invited her neighbor, Mrs. Brown, to her house for coffee. Mrs. Brown is admiring Mrs. Smith's house plants.

Mrs. Brown: You **have** such **a knack for** growing plants. Is it really as easy as you say? What's your secret?

Mrs. Smith: Believe me, if I had one, I'd tell you. The truth is that I don't know. Maybe it's just luck, but I've always been good at growing plants.

Mrs. Brown: I don't understand it! I've tried everything with mine . . . even talking to them, but they're still all dying. I admire your ability.

Mrs. Smith: But I don't do anything special. I just sort of know when they need to be watered and where in the house they get the best sun.

Mrs. Brown: Well, you must be one of those people who **has a green thumb**. Obviously, I'm not. All I can say is that I envy you.

ANALYSIS   Circle the best answer to the question below. Then turn the page and read the explanation for your choice. If you are wrong, choose again.

According to Mrs. Brown, why are Mrs. Smith's plants so healthy?

A.   Mrs. Smith's plants need little attention and care.

B.   Mrs. Smith has a secret that she will not tell.

C.   Mrs. Smith has a natural ability for growing plants.

9

EXPLANATION A. There is no mention of how much time Mrs. Smith devotes to her plants, nor of how much care they require.

B. Mrs. Smith has no secret. She says she would tell Mrs. Brown if she had one.

C. Mrs. Smith has a natural feeling for what plants need. She seems to be able to grow them effortlessly. To **have a green thumb** means to be able to grow things easily. This is the best answer.

ATTITUDE **Mrs. Brown admires the ability to do something with ease.**

EXPANSION A. Put a checkmark (✓) in front of the statements that show ease of effort.

✓   Ann's garden is beautiful. She can make anything grow. Her friends say she **has a green thumb**.

_____ 1. Understanding geometry is no problem for Frank. He thinks it **is a breeze**.

_____ 2. Sue has trouble sewing. She feels the needle is too small and her hands are too big. When she tries to thread a needle, she **is all thumbs**.

_____ 3. Henry cannot dance very well at all. He is always tripping over his partner. Henry **has two left feet**.

_____ 4. Peter always seems to know when I want him to telephone me. He **has a knack for** knowing when to call.

_____ 5. Jan made her first million dollars when she was only nineteen. People say she **has a golden touch**.

_____ 6. Bruce is a good newspaper reporter. He always seems to know where to go for the news. He **has a nose for** a good story.

_____ 7. Mary is very good at standing on her head. For her, it **is easy as pie**.

B. Find the sentence in each of the following that does not fit and cross it out.

Jane **has a green thumb**. ~~Nothing grows in her garden.~~ Her tomatoes are always big and juicy. Her peppers look delicious. She has more green beans than she can use.

1. Mary's exam **was a breeze** for her. She knew all of the answers and she finished before most of the other students. She got the lowest mark in the class. Her teacher was proud of her.

2. Gene **is all thumbs**. One night at a party, he spilled his drink all over himself. Another night, he carried a tray of eggs home from the store without breaking any. Last night, he dropped five plates while doing the dishes.

3. Ken **has a golden touch**. He made a million dollars in real estate and then doubled it overnight in the stock market. He will always have to worry about money. Everything he does makes him richer.

4. Sam **has two left feet**. Everyone wants to dance with him. He is always falling down or stepping on someone's foot. He will never learn to dance.

5. Sue **has a knack for** being in the wrong place at the wrong time. Two years ago, she was on an airplane that was hijacked. Last year, she was in a bank during a robbery. Not too long ago, she was in a restaurant at a table next to her favorite film star. And last week, she was stuck in an elevator for ten hours.

6. For John, learning languages ***is easy as pie***. At the age of ten he could speak English, French, and German. He could speak Spanish well after six months of study. It only took him seven years to learn Portuguese.

7. Phil is a fisherman who ***has a nose for*** knowing where the fish are. He is never wrong. His family had fish for dinner every night last week. Phil never catches anything.

C. Fill in the following with the correct idiom.

Margaret's roses usually take first place in flower competitions. Everyone knows she *has a* _____ green _____ *thumb* .

1. Susan will not have to work a day of her life. She _____ __ _____

    _____ touch .

2. Andy is interested in repairing watches but will never be good at it because

    he _____ all _____ .

3. Steve is not worried about passing his driving test. He thinks it will _____

    _____ easy _____ _____ .

4. Dick usually drives a big truck, so driving a small car _____ __ _____ breeze ___

    for him.

5. Mary is probably the worst dancer in the school because she _____

    _____ _____ _____ feet ___ .

COMMUNICATION   Read and discuss the following:

1. Let's suppose that you work in an employment agency and someone who ***has two left feet*** comes to you looking for a job. Below is a list of openings you would not recommend. Give a reason for each one.

    salesperson in an antique shop   tight-rope walker
    dance teacher   ski instructor

2. Think of five things that you did yesterday. Which ones ***were easy as pie*** and which were not? In each case, give a reason for your answer.

3. A person who ***is all thumbs*** is not good with activities involving skillful use of the hands. For example, this kind of person would not be good at playing the piano. What else would someone who ***is all thumbs*** not be good at doing?

4. To ***have a knack for*** doing something suggests that the ability to do something easily comes naturally. It can have both good and bad consequences. Some people ***have a knack for*** finding their way around a new place, while others ***have a knack for*** getting lost. What other things might people have a knack for doing?

4 Hard Work

Work like a dog

burn the midnight oil
do back-breaking work
fall down on the job
goof off

hit the books
keep one's nose to the grindstone
work like a dog
work one's fingers to the bone

SITUATION   Read the following dialog:

Mr. Bello, the vice president of a computer company, is in his office talking with Mr. Schuman, a departmental supervisor who is retiring soon.

Mr. Bello: Well, John, you're going to be hard to replace. Who do you think would be good for the job?

Mr. Schuman: The most dedicated programmer in the department is Ms. Fagan. She comes in early, often stays late, and does twice as much work as anyone else. I've never seen her *fall down on the job*. A hard worker like that deserves to be considered.

Mr. Bello: It sounds as though she really *works her fingers to the bone*. I see you think very highly of her. Why don't you send her up to see me?

Mr. Schuman: Sure thing, Mr. Bello.

ANALYSIS   Circle the best answer to the question below. Then turn the page and read the explanation for your choice. If you are wrong, choose again.

Why did Mr. Schuman suggest Ms. Fagan for the position of departmental supervisor?

A.   He felt that a woman could do this particular kind of work better than a man.

B.   She has been with the company longer than any other employee.

C.   She works harder than the other employees.

EXPLANATION A. There is nothing in the conversation to indicate that Ms. Fagan is being considered because she is a woman.

B. Sometimes higher positions are offered to employees because of the number of years they have been with the company. However, that is not the case here.

C. Ms. Fagan works seriously and spends long hours at work. This is the best answer.

ATTITUDE **Mr. Schuman feels that hard work should be rewarded.**

EXPANSION A. Carl is a hard worker, but Eric is not. If the sentence below best describes Carl, write his name beside it. If it best describes Eric, write his name.

*Carl*_____ He **works his fingers to the bone**. In other words, he studies hard.

_____ 1. He **burns the midnight oil**. In other words, he studies very late at night.

_____ 2. He **falls down on the job**. In other words, he fails to do well.

_____ 3. He **hits the books**. In other words, he studies in a serious way.

_____ 4. He **goofs off**. In other words, he does not work seriously.

_____ 5. He **does back-breaking work**. In other words, he does very difficult physical work.

_____ 6. He **keeps his nose to the grindstone**. In other words, he works hard all the time.

_____ 7. He **works like a dog**. In other words, he works hard and seriously.

B. Choose the best answer for the following:

_b_ Stan **works his fingers to the bone**.

a. He only uses his hands in his work.
b. He works hard and seriously.
c. He works until he is tired.

_____ 1. Sandy **burned the midnight oil** last night.

a. She was afraid of the dark.
b. She was saving electricity.
c. She was up until 3:00 A.M. because she had an exam the next day.

_____ 2. John **does back-breaking work**.

a. He has huge doctor bills.
b. He works in an office behind a desk.
c. He does demanding physical work.

_____ 3. Sharon often **falls down on the job**.

a. She does not do what is expected of her.
b. She has to stand up a lot on her job.
c. She has accidents on the job.

_____ 4. Mark *keeps his nose to the grindstone*.

     a. He takes three-day weekends.

     b. He never stops working.

     c. He does not work much.

_____ 5. Steve *works like a dog*.

     a. He works with animals.

     b. He works when he wants.

     c. He works hard.

_____ 6. Cathy often *goofs off* at work.

     a. She rarely works seriously.

     b. She often works seriously.

     c. She is a good worker.

_____ 7. John *hit the books* when he was a student.

     a. He got angry when he had to study.

     b. He studied a lot.

     c. He seldom did his assignments.

C. Sally is a success. She worked hard when she was a student and she graduated with honors. She accepted a position with a large company as a sales manager and worked long and hard hours for years. Now she is vice-president in charge of marketing. Using the idioms in the list below, write sentences describing Sally. Some of the sentences will be in the negative, and some in the past tense.

burn the midnight oil	*keep one's nose to the grindstone*
fall down on the job	*work like a dog*
goof off	*work one's fingers to the bone*
hit the books	

Sally never falls down on the job.

_____

_____

_____

_____

_____

_____

COMMUNICATION   Read and discuss the following:

1. People who *work their fingers to the bone* are sometimes accused of not taking time to enjoy life. How can too much work be harmful to the well-being of a person?

2. To show their appreciation for a job well done, employers often give their workers promotions. *The Peter Principle* is a theory which states that these employees eventually reach their "level of incompetence," which means that they are promoted to positions for which they do not qualify. What effect might this phenomenon have on the people involved and on the company?

3. In the United States people who ***do back-breaking work***, such as construction workers, often receive larger paychecks than those people who do not engage in physical labor. Why do you think this is so? Is it the case in your country?

4. Suppose that you are an employer and you are considering hiring someone. You want to use the following list as a guideline, but you know that some of the categories are more important than others. Number the list in order of importance. Compare and discuss your results with your classmates. Be prepared to justify your answers. You may add to the list on the lines provided if you like.

    past experience   friendliness
    age   ethnic background
    appearance   marital status
    sex   dedication
    ability   education and training

    _____   _____

    _____   _____

    _____   _____

Sticks to her guns

5
Compromise

all or nothing
find middle ground
give-and-take
go halfway

meet someone halfway
middle-of-the-road
stick to one's guns

SITUATION   Read the following dialog:

It is seven o'clock in the evening. Mrs. Scheller is at home reading while her children, Tom and Dave, are watching television.

Tom: Mom! I was watching my favorite program and Dave came in and changed the station.

Dave: Tom never lets me watch what I want to.

Mrs. Scheller: Now, boys. We've only got one TV set, so you two are going to have to learn to compromise and **go halfway** with each other. Decide how you want to divide the time.

Tom: Okay. I'll choose the shows until ten and Dave can choose after that.

Dave: No . . . You know we have to go to bed at ten.

Mrs. Scheller: I'd like to see some more **give-and-take** on your part, Tom. You've got to share the TV with your brother.

Tom: Oh, all right. My program is over at eight. If I can finish watching it, then you can have the set.

Dave: Okay.

Mrs. Scheller: Now that's what I like to see. I'll be upstairs if you need me.

ANALYSIS   Circle the best answer to the question below. Then turn the page and read the explanation for your choice. If you are wrong, choose again.

Why was Mrs. Scheller pleased?

A.   It is almost ten o'clock and close to the children's bedtime.

B.   She is able to watch her favorite television program.

C.   Her sons were able to settle their argument by agreeing to share the television.

17

EXPLANATION A. It is seven o'clock, not almost ten. The children have almost three more hours before they have to go to bed.

B. Mrs. Scheller is reading and not watching television.

C. Mrs. Scheller was pleased that her sons were able to reach a compromise. This is the best answer.

ATTITUDE **Mrs. Scheller feels that there are times when it is best to compromise.**

EXPANSION A. Answer with "yes" or "no."

yes Lynn is willing to **go halfway**. She feels that if people do not give a little on their position, nothing will ever get done. She does not think people should be so stubborn that they refuse to change their minds. Does Lynn compromise?

_____ 1. Susie always tries to **find middle ground** in an argument. She does not like extremes. She is comfortable when she is halfway between the two sides of a discussion. Does Susie compromise?

_____ 2. With Mike it is **all or nothing**. If he cannot have everything he wants in the way that he wants it, he would rather not have it at all. Does Mike compromise?

_____ 3. Florence likes to **meet people halfway**. She feels it is important to make decisions that everybody can accept. She will give up part of what she wants for the sake of reaching an agreement. Does Florence compromise?

_____ 4. Ellen **sticks to her guns**. She will not listen to people who say she is wrong. No matter how much others try to get her to see their point of view, once she has formed an opinion, she holds on to it. Does Ellen compromise?

_____ 5. Allan is a **middle-of-the-road** man. He can always see the worth of both sides of the argument. He feels that the best decisions are always between the two opposite points of view. Does Allan compromise?

_____ 6. Henry is for **give-and-take**. He feels that in order to reach an agreement, people have to give up part of what they want. He thinks that if people do that, everybody will benefit. Does Henry compromise?

B. Mr. O'Leary is a political candidate who will compromise in some areas. Make two lists: first of the areas in which he is willing to compromise, and second of the areas in which he is unwilling to compromise.

In tax reform, he will **go halfway**.

1. When it comes to health care, he **sticks to his guns**.
2. In foreign policy matters, he is known for his **give-and-take**.
3. As for capital punishment, it is **all or nothing** for him.
4. When it comes to welfare, he tries to **find middle ground**.
5. As for anti-pollution laws, he is a **middle-of-the-road** candidate.
6. When it comes to law and order, he will **meet his opponents halfway**.

Areas in which Mr. O'Leary is willing to compromise	Areas in which Mr. O'Leary is unwilling to compromise
tax reform	

C.   Some members of the Wright family are willing to compromise, and some are not. This sometimes makes life difficult for all of them. Fill in the blanks with the missing words.

Mr. Wright is willing to __go__ *halfway* .

1.   Mrs. Wright _____ sticks ____ _____ _____ .

2.   Martha, the oldest, tries to _____ _____ _____ ground .

3.   Phil believes in _____ - _____ - _____ take .

4.   Sally is a _____ middle - ____ - _____ - _____ person.

5.   As for Billy, the youngest, it is _____ all ____ _____ .

COMMUNICATION   Read and discuss the following:

1.   In some places, the cost of goods is fixed and shopkeepers will not compromise on the price. In other places, bargaining for goods is common, and the buyer and the seller mutually agree on a price—that is, they **compromise**. Which do you prefer, and why?

2.   If two children are fighting over a piece of pie, their mother might say, "Split it down the middle," meaning that the children should compromise and each take half of the piece of pie. At what other times would a mother say "Split it down the middle"? When would it be inappropriate to say this?

3.   A controversial issue is an issue in which public opinion is divided into opposing sides. What are some controversial issues today? What are the positions taken by the two extremes? What is the **middle-of-the-road** position?

4.   Sometimes people feel so strongly about something that they are unwilling to compromise. Talk about a time when you **stuck to your guns**.

6
Independence

Be tied to one's mother's Apron strings

be a copycat	*cut the apron strings*
be a mama's boy	*have a mind of one's own*
be a yes-man	*lead someone by the nose*
be on one's own	*stand on one's own two feet*
be tied to one's mother's apron strings	

SITUATION Read the following dialog:

Mr. and Mrs. Field are discussing their son, Bill, who will be a college freshman in the fall.

Mrs. Field: I'm a little worried about Bill. He's never been away from home before.

Mr. Field: Well, it has to happen sooner or later. He has to learn to take care of himself and to **stand on his own two feet**.

Mrs. Field: But he's only seventeen . . .

Mr. Field: Evelyn, it'll be good for him. He can't depend on us for the rest of his life. After all, I left home when I was his age, and I did all right. It's time for him to **be on his own**.

Mrs. Field: Oh, I know he has to leave sometime, but I'll still worry.

ANALYSIS Circle the best answer to the question below. Then turn the page and read the explanation for your choice. If you are wrong, choose again.

Why does Mr. Field think that going away to college will be good for Bill?

A. He feels that it is time for his son to support himself.

B. He feels that this will encourage Bill to make decisions for himself.

C. He wants Bill to have a good university education.

EXPLANATION   A.   There is nothing said between Mr. and Mrs. Field that indicates that Mr. Field will no longer support Bill. In fact, he will probably be spending a lot of money to send his son to college.

                    B.   Mr. Field feels that Bill should learn to be independent. This is what he means when he says that Bill should learn to **stand on his own two feet** and to **be on his own**. This is the best answer.

                    C.   Like any parent, Mr. Field would certainly want his son to receive a good education. The focus of the conversation here, however, is on the independence Bill will gain by being away at school.

ATTITUDE   **Mr. Field thinks that people should be independent and make decisions for themselves.**

EXPANSION   A.   Put a "D" in front of the expressions that indicate dependence, and an "I" in front of those that indicate independence.

     _I_   Cindy **is on her own** now. She has graduated from college, gotten a job, and is supporting herself.

            1.   Barbara **has a mind of her own**. She does what she feels is best, even if her friends do not agree with her.

            2.   Grace **is tied to her mother's apron strings**. She cannot do anything without first asking her mother.

            3.   Mary **is a copycat**. Whatever Cheri does, she does.

            4.   Betty lets Bob **lead her by the nose**. She does whatever Bob wants her to do.

            5.   Rob finally **cut the apron strings**. He moved away from home into his own apartment.

            6.   Frank **is a yes-man**. He always does what his boss tells him to, even if he thinks it is a bad idea.

            7.   Little Mike **is a Mama's boy**. Whenever something goes wrong, he runs to his mother.

            8.   Dave has learned to **stand on his own two feet**. He makes all of his decisions now.

                    B.   In the following, Mr. Field is speaking to his son, Bill, Cross out the sentences that do not belong.

~~Son, I am glad you **are a mama's boy**.~~ You are seventeen now and it is time that you **cut the apron strings**. In a few months you will be off to college and **on your own**. I would just like to give you this advice: **Be a yes-man**. Make your own decisions and **stand on your own two feet**. Don't worry about failure. You have to learn to **have a mind of your own**. Always remember to **be led by the nose**. Enjoy yourself, son. Your college days are the best days of your life.

C. John and Jenny Jackson are twins who just celebrated their fourteenth birthday. They are, however, very different. John has never learned to be independent, while Jenny showed signs of independence at a very early age. Using the expressions below, describe John and then Jenny. You may use an expression more than once, and you may put some sentences in the negative.

stand on one's own two feet	*have a mind of one's own*
be a mama's boy	*cut the apron strings*
be tied to one's mother's apron strings	*be a copycat*
be a yes-man	*lead someone by the nose*

John

He does not stand on his own two feet.

Jenny

_____

COMMUNICATION   Read and discuss the following:

1. What do you think is the origin of the expression *stand on your own two feet*?

2. At what age are people generally *on their own* in your country? Is it the same age for males and females?

3. Suppose you are the president of a company. What are the advantages and disadvantages of having *yes-men* work for you?

4. Billy, who is four years old, *has a mind of his own*. What kind of child do you think he is?

7
Honesty/Directness

Be two-faced

bare one's soul
be two-faced
be up front
get something off one's chest
lay one's cards on the table

look someone in the eye
pull the wool over someone's eyes
talk behind someone's back
tell it like it is

SITUATION   Read the following dialog:

John Goodrich is an employee at the Ajax Manufacturing Company. His boss, Mr. Smith, is at home having dinner with his wife.

Mrs. Smith: You're not eating much at all, dear. Aren't you hungry?

Mr. Smith: It's not that. I guess I'm upset over something that happened at work.

Mrs. Smith: Oh?

Mr. Smith: You remember John Goodrich, don't you? I hired him several months ago and I really thought he liked working for us . . .

Mrs. Smith: What do you mean? What happened?

Mr. Smith: Well, he was **talking behind my back**. I was outside his office—he didn't see me, of course—and he was telling another employee how unhappy he was at Ajax.

Mrs. Smith: Why would he do that? Didn't he tell you the other day that he was very happy with his job?

Mr. Smith: Yes . . . But that wasn't what he said to everybody else in the office.

Mrs. Smith: I had no idea he **was** so **two-faced**.

ANALYSIS   Circle the best answer to the question below. Then turn the page and read the explanation for your choice. If you are wrong, choose again.

Why is Mr. Smith upset with John Goodrich?

A.   John is not a good worker.

B.   John was talking instead of working.

C.   John did not come to Mr. Smith with his complaints.

EXPLANATION A. There is no information or evidence that John's work is not good.

B. It is not simply because John was talking, but what he was talking about that upset Mr. Smith.

C. Mr. Smith is upset that John was neither honest nor direct with him. This is the best answer.

ATTITUDE **Mr. Smith prefers people to be honest and direct.**

EXPANSION A. In each of the following, write "yes" if the person is honest and direct. Write "no" if the person is not.

no Bill told Steve that he really liked Steve's girlfriend, Gail. The same day, however, he told Jim that he thought Gail was a bore. Bill *is two-faced*.

_____ 1. Sandy talked to Jill about her most personal problems. Jill now knows just about everything important there is to know about Sandy. Sandy *bared her soul* to Jill.

_____ 2. Mark was allowed to borrow his father's car on the condition that he not take it out of town. Mark drove the car one night to a neighboring town and his father never found out. Mark *pulled the wool over his father's eyes*.

_____ 3. Mary did not do her homework because she had forgotten all about it. She thought she might tell her teacher she had lost it, but she decided to tell him what really happened. She *was up front* with her teacher.

_____ 4. Barb and Maryanne room together. Maryanne often borrows Barb's clothes without asking her. This bothers Barb, but she has not said anything to Maryanne. Finally she tells Maryanne that she has something she *wants to get off her chest*. She tells her what has been bothering her.

_____ 5. Frank Smith is running for governor. In his speeches to the people of his state, he says exactly what he thinks. He hides nothing. Frank Smith *tells it like it is*.

_____ 6. When Mary is with Alice, she often criticizes Bill. When she is with Bill, she often criticizes Alice. Neither Bill nor Alice knows that she does this. Mary often *talks behind her friends' backs*.

_____ 7. Jill made it clear when she had her job interview that although she wanted to work for that company, she was planning to move to another state in a year. She thought it was important for her to *lay her cards on the table*.

_____ 8. Mrs. West's daughter, Joann, broke a lamp while playing with her brother. When Mrs. West asked Joann what happened to the lamp, Joann *looked her mother in the eye* and told her the truth.

B. Mark is well-liked by people because he is very open and frank with them. Walter, however, has few friends because he is the opposite. Below are some comments that people might make about one or the other. Write the name of the person that the sentence best describes.

Walter   He *is two-faced*.

_____ 1. He *tells it like it is*.

_____ 2. He *lays his cards on the table*.

_____ 3. He *bares his soul*.

_____ 4. He likes to *get things off his chest*.

_____ 5. He *is up front*.

_____ 6. He *pulls the wool over people's eyes*.

_____ 7. He *looks people in the eye*.

_____ 8. He *talks behind people's backs*.

C. Fill in the blanks with the appropriate ending from the following list. Pay attention to grammar.

get something off his chest	*tell it like it is*
looking him in the eye	*laid her cards on the table*
is two-faced	*pulled the wool over her mother's eyes*
talking behind her back	*bares her soul*

Bill often tells Sharon one thing and Karen another. He *is* *two-faced* .

1. Mary told me everything. She always _____ _____ to me.

2. Jim was telling stories about Sue, and Sue did not know it. Jim was

_____ .

3. There is something that John has been keeping inside himself for a long time, and he wants to tell it now. He wants to _____

_____ .

4. Sally told her mother that she went to a friend's house, but she really went to a party. Her mother never learned the truth. Sally _____

_____ .

5. My children will not be afraid to tell me what I want to know. They

    _____ .

6. Joan's boss wanted to know exactly what her intentions were, so Joan

    _____ .

7. When Andy gave his explanation, Dick believed it because Andy was

    _____ .

COMMUNICATION   Read and discuss the following:

1. When people **lay their cards on the table**, they are being completely open about something. Explain where this expression comes from.

2. To tell a "little white lie" means that a person tells an untruth in order not to hurt another. Although it appears to contradict the value of honesty and directness, it is acceptable because in a small matter, people do not want to offend someone they know and like. If, for example, you are sick and look terrible, and a friend who visits you says you look wonderful, that person is telling a "little white lie." Can you think of other situations in which a "little white lie" might be appropriate?

3. If you were Mr. Smith in the dialog, how would you handle the problem of John Goodrich talking behind your back?

4. In some countries, **looking someone in the eye** is a way to indicate that people are listening carefully to each other. Is this so in your country? If not, what does direct eye contact communicate?

Give someone the ax

8
Fair Play

add insult to injury
be a good sport
be a hit below the belt
fair shake
get away with murder

get burned
give someone the ax
rake someone over the coals
throw someone a curve

SITUATION Read the following dialog:

Paul's girlfriend, Amy, has just told him that she does not want to see him anymore. Paul is very sad, and he is talking to his friend Rich about it.

Paul: What a surprise! Amy really ***threw me a curve***. All along she said that she liked me, and then suddenly she said that she wanted to break up. I feel terrible.

Rich: That's too bad. I really thought she liked you, too. I wonder what happened . . .

Paul: I don't know. You know what really hurts is that she told me that the only reason she went out with me is that I have a nice car.

Rich: What? How could she say that? That's not fair. That *is* really ***a hit below the belt***.

ANALYSIS Circle the best answer to the question below. Then turn the page and read the explanation for your choice. If you are wrong, choose again.

Why were Paul and Rich so upset with the way Amy ended the relationship?

A. She was too rough on Paul.

B. She broke up with him when he was sick.

C. She hit him.

EXPLANATION   A.   Amy could have ended the relationship in a way that would not have hurt Paul so much. By saying that she only liked his car and not him, she was unfair. This is the best answer.

B.   Paul was not physically ill when Amy broke up with him. He feels terrible now because of the break-up.

C.   There is no indication that Amy physically hit Paul. A ***hit below the belt*** is something done to another in an unfair way.

ATTITUDE   **Paul and Rich feel that people should be fair to one another.**

EXPANSION   A.   Choose the best explanation for the idiom in the sentences below. Answer with "a" or "b."

a   The football coach ***threw Dan a curve***. He assured Dan he would be picked for the team, but in the end, he told him he was not good enough.

   a. The coach misled Dan.
   b. The coach pleasantly surprised Dan.

_____ 1.   When Peter smashed his car, the insurance company gave him a ***fair shake***. They gave him enough money to repair his car.

   a. The insurance company cheated Peter.
   b. The insurance company treated Peter fairly.

_____ 2.   In the divorce settlement, Margaret ***got burned***. Her ex-husband got everything and she got nothing.

   a. Margaret was treated unfairly.
   b. Margaret was treated fairly.

_____ 3.   Chris ***got away with murder***. She knew her parents would not like it, but she stayed out all night at a party. When she got home, her parents did not say anything to her.

   a. Chris was punished for what she did.
   b. Chris was not punished for what she did.

_____ 4.   When Ruth broke Kathy's favorite bowl, Kathy ***raked her over the coals***. She yelled and yelled at Ruth, told her she was clumsy and said that she should never touch anything of hers again.

   a. Kathy criticized Ruth sharply.
   b. Kathy excused Ruth for what she had done.

_____ 5.   When Jean cooked dinner for Nancy, she burned the food. Nancy refused to eat it. To ***add insult to injury***, she told Jean that she was not a good cook, and probably never would be.

   a. Nancy unnecessarily hurt Jean's feelings.
   b. Nancy was trying to help Jean.

_____ 6.   When Terry failed the English test, Kelly told him he was stupid and would never learn to speak English. Kelly's comment ***was a hit below the belt***.

   a. Kelly wanted to make Terry feel better.
   b. Kelly's comment was unfair.

_____ 7. Mr. Erickson, the store manager, **gave Larry the ax**. One day Larry came to work, and with no warning, he was fired.

    a. Larry knew he was going to be fired.

    b. The loss of his job surprised Larry.

_____ 8. Linda and her friends had decided to go to the movies. Linda wanted to see one movie, and everyone else wanted to see another. Linda **was a good sport**, and went to the movie her friends wanted to see.

    a. Linda gracefully accepted the decision of the group.

    b. Linda was angry because her friends did not go to the movie she had chosen.

B. Write "yes" if the conclusion is likely, and "no" if it is unlikely.

no   If Elizabeth says something about Emily that **is a hit below the belt**, she expects Emily to thank her.

_____ 1. If Mr. Stack **gives Joan the ax**, he tells her he is pleased with her work.

_____ 2. If Tim **adds insult to injury**, he is being unkind.

_____ 3. If Margaret **is a good sport**, she complains about losing the game.

_____ 4. If Sally **gets away with murder**, she is punished.

_____ 5. If Andy **rakes Becky over the coals**, he says mean things to her.

_____ 6. If Franny **gives Gerry a fair shake**, she makes him angry.

_____ 7. If Hank **got burned**, he was badly hurt.

_____ 8. If Sylvia **throws Bob a curve**, she does something unpleasant that he does not expect.

C. Make a question for each of the following answers using the appropriate idiom. Pay attention to tense.

add insult to injury	**get burned**
be a hit below the belt	**give someone the ax**
be a good sport	**rake someone over the coals**
fair shake	**throw someone a curve**
get away with murder	

Do you think *that was a hit below the belt* ?

Some people don't think so, but I do. I've never seen anything so unfair in my life.

1. Did you hear _____ ?

I just heard a few minutes ago. Poor Sally. I wonder where she'll work next?

2. Did you know _____ ?

No, I didn't know. It's hard to believe Gene got mad at Ken and criticized him.

3.   Do you think _____?

Yes, I do think so. Johnnie's parents let him do whatever he wants, whenever he wants. They spoil him.

4.   Is Mary _____?

No, she isn't. Mary positively hates to be teased.

5.   Did you _____?

I sure did. I didn't deserve an "F" on that exam.

6.   Did you have to _____?

No, I didn't have to, and I'm sorry I did. Sometimes I don't know when to stop.

7.   Did Mark _____?

Did he ever. Mark promised to help me, but he changed his mind at the last minute. Boy, was I surprised.

8.   Did Ms. Ritcher _____?

Yes, she did. Ms. Richter gave me a "B," and that's the mark I think I should have.

COMMUNICATION   Read and discuss the following:

1.   Some of the expressions in this lesson have their origin in sports, such as **be a hit below the belt, throw someone a curve,** and **be a good sport**. Think of your favorite sport. What is considered fair play? What is not considered fair play?

2.   In the following sentences, some sort of harm has been done to someone. Your job is to make the situation even worse. In other words, **add insult to injury**.

John laughed at Mary's mistake, and then he _____

_____ .

First Don pushed Steve to the ground, and then he _____

_____ .

Sharon told Linda that she did not like her dress, and then she _____

_____ .

3.   Part of the reason that children are encouraged to participate in team sports is to learn the rules of good sportsmanship. Through sports, they gain a sense of fair play. A popular saying in English is, "It's not whether you win or lose, it's how you play the game," meaning that the important thing in achieving something is that you are fair to others while doing it. Although this saying is used in relation to sports, it is used in other contexts as well. For example, people who are looking for a job promotion should not lie, cheat, or hurt others to get that promotion. Do you agree with this saying? Why or why not?

4.   Another popular saying in English is, "All's fair in love and war." Do you agree? Why or why not?

9
Experience

Get one's feet wet

be an old hand at something
be green
be wet behind the ears
get one's feet wet
go to the school of hard knocks

know something like the back of one's hand
know the ropes
live and learn
not be born yesterday

SITUATION Read the following dialog:

Ms. Cooper has invited her friend from the office, Ms. Harding, to have a drink with her at her home after work.

Ms. Cooper: Helen, I've had a leaky faucet for days, and I just can't seem to fix it. I guess I'll have to call a plumber. Do you happen to know any good ones?

Ms. Harding: Let me take a look at it. I know all about plumbing. I **am an old hand at** it.

(ten minutes later)

Ms. Harding: That should do it. It's fine now. If it happens again, just tighten this piece.

Ms. Cooper: I'm impressed, Helen. Where did you ever learn to do that?

Ms. Harding: It comes from lots of practice. My faucets leak all the time.

Ms. Cooper: Well, **live and learn**. Now next time I'll know.

ANALYSIS Circle the best answer to the question below. Then turn the page and read the explanation for your choice. If you are wrong, choose again.

Why was Ms. Cooper impressed that Ms. Harding could repair her faucet?

A. Ms. Harding was strong enough to tighten the piece.

B. She did not know that Ms. Harding was a professional plumber.

C. Ms. Harding knew so much about a skill that Ms. Cooper had never learned.

EXPLANATION A. Ms. Cooper was impressed that Ms. Harding knew how to repair the faucet, not that she was strong enough to repair it.

B. Ms. Harding is not a plumber by profession. She works in an office with Ms. Cooper.

C. Ms. Cooper was impressed with Ms. Harding's knowledge of plumbing. When Ms. Harding said, "*I am an old hand at plumbing*," she meant that she has had considerable experience. This is the best answer.

ATTITUDE **Ms. Cooper recognizes the value of experience.**

EXPANSION A. Put a plus sign (+) in front of the expressions that indicate that a person has had experience, and a minus sign (−) in front of those that indicate the absence of experience.

    +   Ann has been repairing bicycles for years. She *is an old hand at* it.

_____ 1. This is the first time Sue has gone skiing. She will need some help because she *is wet behind the ears*.

_____ 2. Barb has driven to New York so many times that she *knows* the way *like the back of her hand*.

_____ 3. Harry has been working here for a long time. He will show you around. He *knows the ropes*.

_____ 4. You do not have to worry about Frank getting lost. He can take care of himself. Frank *was not born yesterday*.

_____ 5. Mark, an insurance salesman, never went to college, but he knows all there is to know about selling insurance. He *went to the school of hard knocks*.

_____ 6. Yesterday was only Jenny's second time horseback riding. That is why she fell off. She *is* still *green*.

_____ 7. Yesterday Martha started a new job. She *is* just *getting her feet wet*.

_____ 8. Barry, a TV repairman, takes a *live-and-learn* approach in his work. That is why he is good. Every day he knows more about repairing televisions.

B. Cross out the part of the sentence that is the opposite of what the idiomatic expression means.

    Mr. Kepling *is an old hand at* carpentry. He builds very good cabinets, ~~and does not know how to hammer a nail.~~

1. Mr. Riley *knows* the way to the supermarket *like the back of his hand*. He always gets lost going there, and he goes every day.

2. Ms. Pierson *went to the school of hard knocks*. She never received a university degree, and she does not know anything.

3. Mrs. Harrison *was not born yesterday*. She is very naive and she understands what life is all about.

4. Mr. Samuelson *is wet behind the ears*. He is a new member of our club, and he understands all the rules.

5. Miss Harper **knows the ropes**. This is the first time she has painted a room, and she is used to fixing up old houses.

6. Ms. Cramer said, "**Live and learn**." When she washed all of her clothes together, the white ones came out red, but she will probably make the same mistake next time.

7. Dr. Davidson **is green**. He has just graduated from medical school, and he has performed hundreds of operations.

8. Mr. Anderson **is getting his feet wet**. He is learning how to repair his car, and he has done it a thousand times before.

C. Your friend Bill has invited you to go camping with him in the mountains. You want to go, and although you know Bill is an experienced camper, you are a little scared because you have never camped out before. Below, Bill is trying to reassure you. Fill in the blanks with the idioms from the lesson.

Look, don't worry. I _am an_ ___old___ _hand_ at camping. I know you

_____ _____ _____ _____ _____ , but I _____ _____
                                        ears

___ropes___ . We won't get lost. I know the trail_____ _____ _____

_____ ____ ___hand___ . When it comes to camping, I was _____ _____

_____yesterday_____ . After you _____ _____ _____ ___wet___ ,

you'll love it. It's really lots of fun.

COMMUNICATION   Read and discuss the following:

1. The expression **be green**, meaning to be inexperienced, comes from wood that is not aged—wood that is still green. Is the color green associated with inexperience in your country? If not, is the color green associated with something else?

2. It is generally accepted that the older people become, the more experienced they become. However, in the United States there is a law that says that when employees reach the age of seventy, companies can force them to retire, even if they want to continue working. If experience is valued, is this law a contradiction? Why or why not?

3. Almost everybody is **an old hand at** something, such as cooking, gardening, or repairing things. What are you **an old hand at** doing?

4. Riding a bike and driving a car are two things that can only be learned through experience. What others can you think of?

10
Cooperation

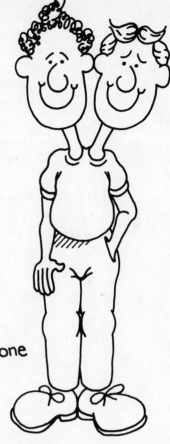

Two heads are better than one

be a loner
brainstorm
go it alone
join forces
lend a hand

pitch in
pool one's resources
put heads together
strike off on one's own
two heads are better than one

SITUATION Read the following dialog:

Sue and Ben are both taking History 101 and their final exam is next week. As they leave class, Ben approaches Sue.

Ben: Hey, Sue . . . I was wondering . . .

Sue: Yeah?

Ben: Well . . . Our final is coming up soon and I was wondering if you would like to study for it together. You know they say that *two heads are better than one*.

Sue: We probably *would* do better if we *joined forces* and studied together. It sounds like it's going to be a real tough exam.

Ben: Is seven o'clock at the library tomorrow night okay with you?

Sue: Fine. I'll meet you outside.

ANALYSIS Circle the best answer to the question below. Then turn the page and read the explanation for your choice. If you are wrong, choose again.

Why does Ben want to study with Sue?

A. He is shy and sees this as a good opportunity to get to know Sue better.

B. He feels he can do a better job on the final exam if he studies with someone else.

C. He will probably fail the exam without Sue's help.

37

EXPLANATION A. Ben does seem indirect with Sue at first. Although this might be a sign of shyness, we have no information that his interest in Sue is anything more than to study with her.

B. Ben feels that his chances of receiving a better grade on the exam would be increased by studying with someone. This is the best answer.

C. Although Sue said the exam would probably be difficult, we are given no information as to what mark Ben might receive if he studies by himself.

ATTITUDE **Ben and Sue feel that cooperation increases the possibility of success.**

EXPANSION A. Write "individual" in front of the sentences that indicate individual effort. Write "group" in front of those that indicate group effort.

group   If Mary **joins forces** with Paul, it means she works with him so that they both achieve what they want.

_____ 1. If Dick **is a loner**, it means that he avoids the company of others and prefers to work by himself.

_____ 2. If Jan **brainstorms** with Al, it means she confers with him to solve a problem.

_____ 3. If Randy wants to **go it alone**, it means he wants to do something by himself.

_____ 4. If Dave **lends** Tom **a hand**, it means he helps him.

_____ 5. If Karen **pools her resources** with others, it means she combines her strengths with them.

_____ 6. If Kathy **pitches in**, it means she helps someone with something.

_____ 7. If Ken and Gene **put their heads together**, it means they work as a team to solve a problem.

_____ 8. If Larry **strikes off on his own**, it means he leaves others in order to do something by himself.

_____ 9. If Barb works with Jean because **two heads are better than one**, it means that by working together they can achieve more than if they work separately.

B. You are forming a study group. Circle the names of the people below who might be interested in belonging.

(Barb) likes to **join forces** with others.

1. George **is a loner**.
2. Mary likes to **pitch in**.
3. Karen likes to **pool her resources** with others.
4. Paul would rather **go it alone**.
5. Tom always says that **two heads are better than one**.
6. Sue thinks it is a good idea to **join forces**.
7. Jim usually **strikes off on his own**.
8. Bill can be counted on to **lend a hand**.
9. Sally likes to **brainstorm** with her classmates.

C. Using the list, write the appropriate ending for each of the following sentences. Pay attention to grammar. There are two sections.

> *is a loner*   *put their heads together*
> *lent a hand*   *to go it alone*
> *two heads are better than one*

1. Sandy and Alice decided to study together because _____*two*_____ *heads are better than one* .

2. Sue saw that Ann was having trouble carrying her heavy suitcase, so she

   _____ .

3. Mark does not have any friends and he spends most of his time by himself

   because he _____ .

4. Joe often works with others, but this time he decided _____

   _____ .

5. Neither Bob nor John could do their algebra homework alone, but they had

   better luck when they _____ .

■■

> *pitched in*   *joins forces with someone*
> *pooled their resources*   *brainstorm with each other*
> *strike off on her own*

6. Sally sometimes would rather work by herself, so no one was surprised

   when she said she wanted to _____ .

7. Ken has been working for an hour on a physics problem and he does not

   think he will ever find the answer unless he _____ .

8. Steve has the money and Mary has the business experience. Together they

   could open a restaurant if they _____ .

9. Karen figured it would take three hours for her to clean up the house, but it

   would take only thirty minutes if her roommates _____ .

10. Ben and Phil are sure they will have a better chance of passing the exam if

    they _____ .

COMMUNICATION   Read and discuss the following:

1. In addition to meaning "help someone," **pitch in** also means "throw in." On many public trash cans across the United States, "**Pitch in**" is written. Explain why both definitions are appropriate.

2. "United we stand; divided we fall" was said by Americans fighting for their independence from England. The Americans knew that if they did not cooperate with each other, they would not win the war. The expression has survived to the present day and is used in many contexts. Give an example of when this expression could be used.

3. Are there times when you like to **go it alone**, that is, do something by yourself? When are they?

4. Let's suppose that your class has been given a very difficult assignment. You decide that it would be to your advantage to **join forces** with a classmate. What might you say to a classmate to convince him or her that if you **pool your resources**, it would be better?

11
Improbability of
Desired Outcome

Cannot change
a leopard's spots

be a long shot
be like looking for a needle in a
  haystack
be out of one's hands
beat the odds
cannot change a leopard's spots

cards stacked against one
hand is dealt
have a snowball's chance in hell
see the writing on the wall
tie one's hands (usually used in the
  passive)

SITUATION   Read the following dialog:

Tom, Patti, and Jo are playing with water pistols on the beach. Jo shoots at Tom, who is
wearing contact lenses. Here is what happens next.

Tom: Wait! Wait! No fair shooting at the face!

Jo: Got ya!

Tom: Hey! Time out. Really. I think I lost a contact. Help me look for it.

(after some time)

Patti: It's not anywhere. We'll never find it. In all that sand, it'd **be like looking for
a needle in a haystack**.

Tom: Patti's right. It would be a waste of time to continue. We **have a snowball's
chance in hell** of finding it. Let's go home.

ANALYSIS   Circle the best answer to the question below. Then turn the page and read the
explanation for your choice. If you are wrong, choose again.

Why did Tom and his friends stop looking for the contact lens?

A.   They decided that the chance of finding it was extremely small.

B.   It was getting colder and it began to snow.

C.   Tom could see fairly well without the lens.

41

EXPLANATION   A.   Tom and his friends decided that the search would probably be a waste of time because the contact was small and because the sand made it difficult to see. This is the best answer.

B.   Tom mentions a snowball, but not in the context of the weather. To **have a snowball's chance in hell** of finding the contact means there is no chance at all of finding it.

C.   Because he wears contact lenses, we know that Tom does not have perfect vision. Beyond that, we have no idea how good or bad his eyes are.

ATTITUDE   **Tom and his friends think it is important to recognize when a desired outcome is unlikely or impossible.**

EXPANSION   A.   Below are several situations that deal with what somebody would like to happen. Each situation is then followed by a question. Answer the question with "yes" or "no."

_no_   Sam has missed a lot of classes and he failed all of his exams. In other words, he **has a snowball's chance in hell** of passing the course. Do you think Sam studied?

_____ 1.   Mark would like a promotion, but he knows his name is not on the list of people being considered. In other words, he **sees the writing on the wall**. Do you think Mark's boss is pleased with his work?

_____ 2.   Sue wanted to lend Mike some money, but she did not have any to give him. In other words, **her hands were tied**. Do you think Sue would lend him the money if she had some?

_____ 3.   Mr. O'Toole, 65, does not want to retire, but the company he works for wants to replace him with a younger person. In other words, it **is out of Mr. O'Toole's hands**. Do you think Mr. O'Toole would continue working if he had a choice?

_____ 4.   Lucy is going to ask her boss for a raise even though she knows that business has not been good lately. In other words, she knows it **is a long shot**. Is it likely that Lucy will get the raise?

_____ 5.   Joan is running for president of the student council, but she is competing with two others who are better qualified for the position than she is. Joan has never been on the student council. In other words, the **cards are stacked against her**. Do you think Joan will win the election?

_____ 6.   Ted went to the racetrack and bet all of his money on a horse that has never won a race. Ted had a feeling that today the horse would come in first. In other words, he tried to **beat the odds**. Do you think Ted's chances of winning were small?

_____ 7.   Gary made a serious mistake at work and his manager fired him. Gary did everything he could to get rehired, but his manager would not listen to him. In other words, the **hand was dealt**. Do you think Gary was able to change his manager's mind?

_____ 8.   Alice forgets everything. She promised her friend, Ann, that she would remember to bring the theater tickets, but when they met to go to the play, Alice realized that she had forgotten them. In other words, you **cannot change a leopard's spots**. Do you think Ann should have been responsible for bringing the tickets instead of Alice?

_____ 9.   Jenny was in her backyard raking leaves and had gathered a huge pile of them when she noticed she had lost an earring. She was sure the earring was in the pile of leaves, so she started looking for it. However, she stopped after fifteen minutes because she knew she probably would not find it. In other words, it **was like looking for a needle in a haystack**. Do you think Jenny's chances of finding her earring were good?

B.   The following are a series of exchanges between two people. Choose the best reply to the first statement.

B.   "She **has a snowball's chance in hell** of getting the job."

    A.   "Yes, she is very qualified."
    B.   "Yes, her chances are pretty poor."

_____ 1.   "It **will be like looking for a needle in a haystack**."

    A.   "Well, let's try anyhow."
    B.   "In that case, it should be easy to find."

_____ 2.   "The **hand is dealt**."

    A.   "We can change it tomorrow."
    B.   "Yes, it's too late to change anything now."

_____ 3.   "It **was a long shot**, but he won."

    A.   "Yeah, everyone knew he was going to win."
    B.   "Yeah, everyone is surprised."

_____ 4.   "You **can't change a leopard's spots**."

    A.   "Yeah, we just have to accept him like he is."
    B.   "I guess we'll try to convince him."

_____ 5.   "The **cards are stacked against me**."

    A.   "Yeah, you'll probably get it."
    B.   "You really don't have much of a chance."

_____ 6.   "He **beat the odds**."

    A.   "I knew he would lose."
    B.   "How much did he win?"

_____ 7.   "**My hands are tied**."

    A.   "Yeah, you can't do anything about it."
    B.   "I'm glad you could help out."

_____ 8.   "I **saw the writing on the wall**."

    A.   "I'm so happy for you."
    B.   "Too bad it didn't work out in your favor."

_____ 9.   "It **is out of her hands** now."

    A.   "You're right. There's nothing she can do."
    B.   "You're right. She will probably keep trying."

C. Mrs. Smith just came home from work and discovered that one of her windows had been broken. Among the pieces of glass on the floor was a baseball. This is the third time this month this has happened. She is furious and decides to insist that the police do something. Below is the phone conversation she has with Police Sergeant O'Malley. Using the idioms from this lesson, fill in the missing words.

Mrs. Smith: You've got to find the kid this time, Sergeant. Enough is enough.

O'Malley: Do you realize what you are asking us to do? There must be five hundred kids in your neighborhood. Finding the one who did it would __be *like looking for a*__ needle __*in a haystack*__ . Besides, it is _____ ____ _____ ____ hands . We get calls like this all the time and the captain told us not to waste our time if the caller did not have any idea who did it.

Mrs. Smith: Don't tell me that your ___ hands _____ _____ . You must have at least one officer who can spare one hour to check this out. I know it ____ __ _____ ____ shot , but you can at least try.

O'Malley: A long shot? Why, we don't ___ have __ __ _____ _____ ____ hell of finding the kid.

Mrs. Smith: I'm beginning to _____ _____ _____ ____ _____ _____ wall . You won't help me, will you?

O'Malley: I'm sorry, Mrs. Smith. If you could give us a description or something, we would be happy to investigate. As it is, the _____ _____ stacked _____ _____ us. It would be a waste of our time to look.

COMMUNICATION   Read and discuss the following:

1. The expression ***the hand is dealt*** comes from the game of cards. A "hand" is the number of cards held by a player; "to deal" means to distribute the cards. Under what circumstances might someone say, "***The hand is dealt?***"

2. An analogy is a relationship between two things that are otherwise different. Learning a language is different from playing the piano, but learning a language is like playing a piano because both require practice in order for someone to be good at them. So, "Learning a language is like playing the piano" is an analogy. Make several analogies that end with "... ***is like looking for a needle in a haystack***."

3. The following is the beginning of a list of situations in which people try to ***beat the odds***. Add to this list.
   Poker
   Horse racing

   _____

   _____

   _____

4. Many countries have lotteries that help pay for programs that otherwise would not have any money. People buy lottery tickets because they hope to win a lot of money, even though the chance of winning is small. Does your country have a lottery? If so, what programs does it support? If your country does not have a lottery, would you like it to have one? Why or why not?

12 Friendliness

Get up on the wrong side of the bed

be cool toward someone
get up on the wrong side of the bed
give someone the cold shoulder
have a bone to pick with someone
have a sunny disposition

icy stare
leave a bad taste in one's mouth
turn one's back on someone
turn one's nose up at someone
welcome someone with open arms

SITUATION   Read the following dialog:

Dick and Jane, brother and sister, are at the breakfast table. Jane has prepared breakfast.

Dick: Jane, I **have a bone to pick** with you. I'm really mad.

Jane: What is it?

Dick: I told you that you could borrow my bike yesterday, but you left it outside last night, and it rained. Why didn't you put it in the garage?

Jane: I'm sorry, Dick. You're right. I should have put it away. It won't happen again.

Dick: These eggs are terrible! What did you do to them?

Jane: Nothing different. Just eat them.

Dick: And the coffee's cold. Why didn't you heat it up?

Jane: Boy, you certainly **got up on the wrong side of the bed** this morning! Just because you're in a bad mood, don't yell at me. Just leave me alone.

ANALYSIS   Circle the best answer to the question below. Then turn the page and read the explanation for your choice. If you are wrong, choose again.

Why did Jane tell Dick not to bother her anymore?

A.   She was ashamed that she had left the bike outside.

B.   Dick was being unpleasant.

C.   She was in a bad mood because she had to make breakfast.

EXPLANATION A. It is true that Jane was sorry that she did not put the bike inside, but this is not why she told Dick to leave her alone.

B. Dick had nothing nice to say to Jane, so she told him not to talk to her. This is the best answer.

C. Although Dick was irritable, there is no indication that Jane minded making breakfast for him.

ATTITUDE **Jane likes people to be friendly.**

EXPANSION A. Put "yes" if the behavior is friendly and you would like to be treated in this way, and "no" if the behavior is unfriendly and you would not like to be treated in this way.

_no_   You are spending the day with one of your classmates, John. Usually, he is very pleasant to be with. However, today nothing anyone does seems to please him. You do not know why he is acting the way he is. You suppose he **got up on the wrong side of the bed** today.

_____ 1. You and your friends, Hank and Mary, are having a cup of coffee together. Hank turns away from you to talk to Mary. He **turns his back on** you.

_____ 2. You are walking down the street and see Mike, a person you work with. You greet Mike pleasantly, but he **gives you the cold shoulder** and walks past you without saying hello.

_____ 3. You are visiting a new city for the first time. You telephone some people you know who live there. They invite you to dinner, and **welcome you with open arms**.

_____ 4. You are at a party and see a classmate. You wave to him across the room, but he **turns his nose up at** you and does not wave back.

_____ 5. Your good friend Sally is introducing her new boyfriend, Frank, to you. You shake hands with him, and try to make conversation, but notice that he **is cool toward** you and does not seem interested in talking with you.

_____ 6. You meet your friend, Amy, and she looks happy to see you. In fact, she is always glad to see you. She **has** such **a sunny disposition**.

_____ 7. You are in the school cafeteria and one of your teachers approaches you and says he **has a bone to pick with** you. He seems angry and looks as though he wants to talk to you about something you did that he did not like.

_____ 8. You see someone that you met a week earlier, Jill. You like her and thought she liked you, but when you greet her, she gives you an **icy stare**. You thought she would be happy to see you. You do not know what went wrong.

_____ 9. Your friend Bill has been trying to talk you into refusing a particular summer job. When you see your friend Jack, he tells you that Bill told him he wants the job for himself. What Jack says **leaves a bad taste in your mouth**.

B. In many U.S. high schools, students in the graduating senior class are recognized by their classmates for certain of their qualities. Someone may be chosen "The Most Likely To Succeed"; another may be chosen "The Best Athlete." Still another may be chosen "The Most Popular." The candidates for this last category must be friendly. Circle the name in the sentences below if the person might be a good choice for "The Most Popular." Cross out the name if the person would not.

S̶h̶e frequently ***has a bone to pick with*** someone.

1. John ***is often cool toward*** his friends.

2. Mary even ***gives her best friends the cold shoulder*** from time to time.

3. Jim never ***gets up on the wrong side of the bed***.

4. Karen always ***has a sunny disposition***.

5. Margaret's ***icy stares*** could freeze a polar bear.

6. Mark's actions sometimes ***leave a bad taste in his friends' mouths***.

7. Sandy ***turns her back on*** just about everyone.

8. Barb would never ***turn her nose up at*** anyone.

9. Lesley always ***welcomes her friends with open arms***.

C. Alice is angry at her friend, Mary Ann. The next time she sees her, she is going to do something to show Mary Ann that she is not happy with her. Below are some possibilities. Finish the sentences with the appropriate idiom.

Alice could tell Mary Ann that she *has* a *bone* *to* _____ pick *with* _____ her.

1. Alice could _____ Mary Ann _____ cold _____ .

2. Alice could _____ cool _____ Mary Ann.

3. Alice could give Mary Ann _____ icy _____ .

4. Alice could _____ _____ back _____ Mary Ann.

5. Alice could _____ _____ nose _____ at Mary Ann.

6. Alice could tell Mary Ann that she _____ left ___ _____ _____
    _____ _____ mouth _____ .

COMMUNICATION   Read and discuss the following:

1.   In English, the sun is associated with warmth, cheerfulness, and friendliness. This is the origin of the expression **have a sunny disposition**. In your language, what adjectives are associated with the sun?

2.   To **welcome someone with open arms**, to **turn one's back on** someone, and to **turn one's nose up at** someone all refer to ways that the body communicates friendliness or unfriendliness. What other body gestures can you think of that suggest friendliness or unfriendliness?

3.   Tell about a time when you **had a bone to pick with** someone—in other words, a time when somebody did something you did not like and you wanted to talk to that person about it.

4.   "A smile goes a long way" is a popular English saying which means that people are more likely to get what they want if they are friendly. For instance, shopkeepers who are friendly to their customers and who often smile are likely to get more business than those who are unfriendly and never smile. Can you think of a time when a smile made a difference?

Walk on Air

be down in the dumps
be in seventh heaven
be on cloud nine
be on top of the world
be out of sorts
be tickled pink

feel blue
feel like a million bucks
*look like one has the weight of the
    world on one's shoulders*
look like one lost one's best friend
walk on air

SITUATION Read the following dialog:

It is early May. Marge is talking to her good friend Kate on the phone.

Marge: Have you heard the news?

Kate: No. What?

Marge: Helen and Dick are engaged!

Kate: No kidding? How exciting! Helen has been waiting for this moment for years. She must be very happy.

Marge: You said it. She **is on cloud nine**. She can't stop smiling.

Kate: Well, that's wonderful news. I **am tickled pink** for her. When is the wedding?

Marge: The fifteenth of June.

Kate: That doesn't give them a lot of time to get ready.

Marge: Yeah, I know. Listen, I'll talk to you later. I want to call Nancy and tell her about it, too.

ANALYSIS Circle the best answer to the question below. Then turn the page and read the explanation for your choice. If you are wrong, choose again.

How does Helen feel about marrying Dick?

A. She is worried that she will not have enough time to prepare for the wedding.

B. She is excited because someone is finally going to marry her.

C. She is delighted to be marrying Dick.

51

EXPLANATION   A.   Both Kate and Marge feel there is not a lot of time for preparations, but they do not say there is not enough time. We do not know how Helen feels about it.

B.   Helen is excited that she is marrying Dick, but she would not marry just anybody.

C.   We know that Helen is extremely happy to be marrying Dick because Marge says she *is on cloud nine*. This is the best answer.

ATTITUDE   **Helen's friends feel that happiness is a desirable state.**

EXPANSION   A.   Put a plus sign (+) if the person mentioned is happy. Put a minus sign (−) if the person is sad.

_+_   Steve was accepted at all the universities he applied to. He *is on cloud nine*.

_____ 1.   Jan failed her math exam. She *is down in the dumps* today.

_____ 2.   Bob's parents gave him a trip to Europe for a graduation present. He *is in seventh heaven*.

_____ 3.   Mary came in first in a ten-mile race. She *is on top of the world*.

_____ 4.   Sue does not feel well today. She *is out of sorts*.

_____ 5.   John lost his dog the other day. He *is feeling blue*.

_____ 6.   Karen likes her new car very much. In fact, she *is tickled pink* with it.

_____ 7.   Rich came back from vacation looking great. He says he *feels like a million bucks*.

_____ 8.   Sally lost her job and does not know how she is going to pay her bills. She *looks like she has the weight of the world on her shoulders*.

_____ 9.   Ken got some bad news in the mail today. He *looks like he lost his best friend*.

_____ 10.   Gene found the travelers checks he had lost. He *is walking on air*.

B.   Mark is a very moody person. Some days he is happy and some days he is unhappy. Put "h" next to the days Mark was happy, and "u" next to the days he was unhappy.

_h_   On Sunday, Mark *was tickled pink*.

_____ 1.   On Monday, he *was feeling blue*.

_____ 2.   The next day, he *was walking on air*.

_____ 3.   On Wednesday, he *was down in the dumps*.

_____ 4.   On the following day, he *was out of sorts*.

_____ 5.   On Friday, he *was on top of the world*.

_____ 6.   The day after that, he *felt like a million bucks*.

_____ 7. On Sunday, he *looked like he had lost his best friend*.

_____ 8. The next day, he *looked like he had the weight of the world on his shoulders*.

_____ 9. On Tuesday, he *was on cloud nine*.

_____ 10. On the following day, he *was in seventh heaven*.

C. Jim is the captain of the Jefferson High School basketball team. Walt is the captain of the basketball team at Washington High School. Last week the two teams played each other, and although it was a close game, Jefferson won. Using all of the idioms below, write sentences describing how both Jim and Walt felt after the game. Remember to use the past tense.

be down in the dumps	*be tickled pink*
be in seventh heaven	*feel blue*
be on cloud nine	*feel like a million bucks*
be on top of the world	*look like one lost one's best friend*
be out of sorts	*walk on air*

Jim   Walt

Jim was on cloud nine. _____

_____   _____

_____   _____

_____   _____

_____   _____

_____   _____

_____   _____

_____   _____

_____   _____

COMMUNICATION   Read and discuss the following:

1. The following is a phone conversation between Phil and Al. We know how they are feeling today, but we do not know why. In the spaces provided, supply a possible reason for the way each is feeling.

    Phil: Hello, Al? This is Phil. How are you doing?

    Al: Great! I *feel like a million bucks*.

    Phil: No kidding. Why?

    Al: _____

    _____ . How are you doing?

    Phil: Not so good. I *am* really *down in the dumps* because _____

    _____

    _____

    Al: I am sorry to hear you *are feeling so blue*. Listen, I'll give you a call

    tomorrow to see how you are doing.

    Phil: Okay, thanks. Bye now.

    Al: Bye.

2. Make up a short verse beginning with, "Happiness is . . ." The poem below is an example.

    Happiness is cookies.
    Happiness is cake.
    The only trouble with them is
    They take too long to bake.

3. People the world over celebrate happy occasions. Some of these celebrations may include: births, birthdays, marriages, wedding anniversaries, the new year, religious and national holidays. Choose one of these occasions and tell how it is celebrated in your country.

4. A diary is a written record of what you do every day and how you feel about it. Write a diary yourself, telling how you felt each of the last seven days. Use expressions from the lesson.

Eat like a horse

bite off more than one can chew
burn oneself out
drink like a fish
eat like a horse
eyes are bigger than one's stomach
lose one's head

make a pig out of oneself
run oneself ragged
spread oneself too thin
talk until one is blue in the face
take it easy

SITUATION   Read the following dialog:

It is the day before the big game. Jim, the star basketball player at Parkersburg High School, is still practicing after the rest of the team has left. Mr. Palmer, his coach, is passing through the gym on his way home and sees him.

Coach Palmer: Jim, you've practiced enough. I want you to **take it easy** tonight. You know you should get plenty of rest before the big game tomorrow. It's going to be a tough one.

Jim: I'm too nervous to do anything else, coach. Can't I stay and work out some more?

Coach Palmer: You **are running yourself ragged**. Save some of that energy for tomorrow, Jim. If you push yourself too hard, you won't be any good for the game.

Jim: Okay, coach. You're the boss.

ANALYSIS   Circle the best answer to the question below. Then turn the page and read the explanation for your choice. If you are wrong, choose again.

Why does Coach Palmer want Jim to stop practicing?

A.   He has to lock the gym and go home.

B.   He is afraid that Jim will be too tired to play at his best in tomorrow's game.

C.   He feels that extra practice is not necessary because he is certain of winning the game.

EXPLANATION A. We know that the coach is on his way home, but we do not know if he must go home. Also, we do not know if it is his responsibility to lock the gym.

                        B. The coach wants Jim to be well-rested for tomorrow's game. He is afraid that if Jim keeps practicing, he will be too tired to play well. This is the best answer.

                        C. The coach said that the game will be tough, meaning that it will be difficult to win.

ATTITUDE **Coach Palmer feels that people should know their limitations and not exceed them.**

EXPANSION A. Choose the most likely answer, A or B.

A.   Alice is working much too hard. She is ***running herself ragged***.

        A. Alice is doing too much.
        B. Alice is not doing enough.

_____ 1. Steve asked for more than he could eat. His ***eyes were bigger than his stomach***.

        A. Steve thought he could eat a lot.
        B. Steve did not think he could eat much.

_____ 2. Eric became so upset that he lost control of himself. He ***lost his head***.

        A. Eric was rational.
        B. Eric was irrational.

_____ 3. Jan tried to do more than she had time for. She ***bit off more than she could chew***.

        A. Jan is lazy.
        B. Jan is ambitious.

_____ 4. Stan consumes too many alcoholic beverages. He ***drinks like a fish***.

        A. Stan spends a lot of time in bars.
        B. Stan dislikes bars.

_____ 5. Daniel eats more than anybody else I know. He ***eats like a horse***.

        A. Daniel does not spend a lot of money on food.
        B. Daniel spends a lot of money on food.

_____ 6. Polly did too many things and got over-tired. She ***burned herself out***.

        A. Polly works hard.
        B. Polly does not like to work.

_____ 7. Ken talked and talked, but he did not change Gene's mind. He ***talked until he was blue in the face***.

        A. Ken did not convince Gene.
        B. Gene agreed with Ken.

_____ 8. Franny got involved in too many activities at once. She ***spread herself too thin***.

        A. Franny had enough time to do everything she wanted.
        B. Franny did not have enough time to do everything she wanted.

_____ 9. Helen ate too much. She **made a pig out of herself**.

    A. It was enjoyable to watch Helen eat.

    B. It was not enjoyable to watch Helen eat.

_____ 10. Brian is reading a newspaper under a tree in the park. Brian is **taking it easy**.

    A. Brian is relaxing.

    B. Brian is hard at work.

B.   Choose the idiom that matches the situation.

_**B.**_   Jack spent the weekend fishing.

    A. Jack **burned himself out**.

    B. Jack **took it easy**.

_____ 1. Betty ordered five things from the menu, but could eat only three of them.

    A. Betty's **eyes were bigger than her stomach**.

    B. Betty **drank like a fish**.

_____ 2. Linda joined seven clubs in one week. She never has time for her studies.

    A. Linda **is spreading herself too thin**.

    B. Linda **is taking it easy**.

_____ 3. Ted was so mad at Joe that he beat him up. Later, he was sorry.

    A. Ted **ran himself ragged**.

    B. Ted **lost his head**.

_____ 4. Veronica constantly tries to convince her friends that nuclear energy is good. She tries and tries, but they do not agree with her.

    A. Veronica **is spreading herself too thin**.

    B. Veronica **talks until she is blue in the face**.

_____ 5. Al had four hamburgers, two milkshakes, three orders of French fries, and three apples for lunch.

    A. Al **made a pig out of himself**.

    B. Al **burned himself out**.

_____ 6. Sam is taking five courses, working forty hours a week, and is president of two clubs.

    A. Sam **lost his head**.

    B. Sam **bit off more than he could chew**.

_____ 7. Jenny has five children, works full-time, and takes courses at night. She gets up at 5:00 A.M. and does not go to bed until after midnight.

    A. Jenny **is running herself ragged**.

    B. Jenny's **eyes are bigger than her stomach**.

_____ 8. Kim always has a beer in her hand.

    A. Kim **is burning herself out**.

    B. Kim **drinks like a fish**.

C. Monica, a good friend of yours, tries to do too many things at once. She does not know her limitations. You see that she is always tired and anxious, and you are worried about her. One day, you sit down with her and try to convince her to slow down. Using the expressions below, write out what you would say.

> **bite off more than one can chew**   **take it easy**
> **burn oneself out**   **spread oneself too thin**
> **run oneself ragged**

"Monica, you have to slow down. You can't do everything that you want to do. You are running yourself ragged.

COMMUNICATION Read and discuss the following:

1. Several of the expressions in this lesson compare people to animals, such as "She ***drinks like a fish***," "He ***eats like a horse***," and "She ***is making a pig out of herself***." There are many other expressions in English that compare human traits to animals, such as "wise as an owl," "sly as a fox," and "timid as a mouse." Are there expressions in your language that compare humans to animals? What are they?

2. Look at the following sentences. After each one, someone might say, "Be careful you don't ***spread yourself too thin***."

    "I have to take seven courses this semester."
    "I have four meetings scheduled for tonight."

    Think of other sentences like these.

3. When people ***lose their heads***, they become so upset that they lose control and do or say things they later regret. This happens to almost everybody. For instance, if a man breaks all of the windows in his home because he had a bad day at work, he ***lost his head***. Talk about a time when you ***lost your head*** or when someone you know ***lost his (or her) head***.

16
Control of Emotions

Hold one's head up

be cool as a cucumber
be tough as nails
be tough-skinned
come apart at the seams
fall apart
flip out

go to pieces
hold one's head up
keep a stiff upper lip
keep one's chin up
not bat an eyelash
pull oneself together

SITUATION   Read the following dialog:

Harriet Gold telephones Elsie Wilcott to tell her about the death of Betty Robinson's husband. The three women are all members of the same garden club, but Harriet and Elsie did not know Betty's husband well.

Harriet: Elsie, did you hear that George Robinson passed away last night?

Elsie: Oh my goodness! I knew he was in the hospital, but I didn't know it was that serious. How's Betty holding up?

Harriet: Betty is a brave person. She ***is keeping a stiff upper lip.*** I don't know how she does it. If I were her, I wouldn't be able to stop the tears.

Elsie: Me neither. But like you said, Betty ***is tough as nails***. She never lets it show when things go wrong. I really admire her. Thanks for letting me know, Harriet. I think I'll give Betty a call now and see if there's anything I can do.

ANALYSIS   Circle the best answer to the question below. Then turn the page and read the explanation for your choice. If you are wrong, choose again.

In the eyes of her friends, how is Betty reacting to the death of her husband?

A.   She will not accept the fact that her husband has died.

B.   She is so sad that she cannot stop crying.

C.   She is not showing how she feels.

EXPLANATION A. Although Betty is not showing how she feels, that does not necessarily mean that she does not accept the fact that her husband has died.

B. It is Harriet and Elsie who say that they would not be able to stop crying if they were in Betty's place. Betty's behavior, however, is exactly the opposite.

C. Although Betty is certainly very sad, she is not showing her emotions. This is the best answer.

ATTITUDE **Harriet and Elsie admire people who can control their emotions when things go wrong.**

EXPANSION A. While Mr. and Mrs. Drummer and their six children were on vacation, their house burned down and they lost everything. Here is how the family members and their relatives reacted when they heard the news. Put a plus sign (+) next to those who were able to control how they felt, and a minus sign (−) next to those who were not.

_+_   Mrs. Drummer **kept a stiff upper lip**. She was very brave, and set an example for the rest of the family.

____ 1. Mr. Drummer **kept his chin up**. Like his wife, he was very courageous. He knew his family expected him to be very strong.

____ 2. Hank Drummer **came apart at the seams**. He was afraid the family would never recover its loss. He was so upset that nobody could approach him.

____ 3. Unlike her brother Hank, Patti **was cool as a cucumber**. She knew that they would be able to rebuild the house, and she remained very calm.

____ 4. Mike, the oldest, **was tough-skinned**. He did not cry at all. He comforted his little brothers and sisters.

____ 5. Little Danny Drummer **flipped out**. He was so frightened that he screamed and screamed.

____ 6. Susie **held her head up**. She knew family life would be hard for a while, but she knew her family would be all right. She was not afraid of the future.

____ 7. Brian Drummer **has** always **been tough as nails**. He accepted the news very calmly.

____ 8. When he first heard the news, Grandfather Drummer **did not bat an eyelash**. He never lets people know when he is upset.

____ 9. Uncle Bob **fell apart**. He knew how much the Drummers loved their house. He felt so badly for them that he could not stop crying.

____ 10. At first, Aunt Sally was so shocked that she could not speak. Then she **pulled herself together**. She knew the Drummers would need her help, so she made herself calm down.

____ 11. Grandmother Drummer **went to pieces**. She was so upset that grandfather thought she was going to get sick.

B. Write "yes" next to the sentence if the person controlled his or her emotions, and "no" if the person did not.

yes   When the other children made fun of Annie because her dress was torn, she ***was tough as nails***.

_____ 1. When the judge told the defendant that he was sentenced to twenty years in prison, the defendant ***did not bat an eyelash***.

_____ 2. When Mrs. Skelley heard that her son was in a bad automobile accident, she ***went to pieces***.

_____ 3. When Henry's fiancee said that she did not want to marry him after all, Henry ***kept a stiff upper lip***.

_____ 4. When the doctor told John that he had to have open heart surgery, John ***came apart at the seams***.

_____ 5. When the teacher told Beth that she had failed the course, Beth ***kept her chin up***.

_____ 6. Even though Mr. Kidder was very much in debt, he tried to ***hold his head up*** in public.

_____ 7. Although the crowd disliked his speech and called him names, Senator Thompson ***was cool as a cucumber***.

_____ 8. When Ms. Bradshaw was fired from a job she had had for twenty-five years, she ***fell apart***.

_____ 9. When Mrs. Jennings's two-year-old son got lost in the park, she ***flipped out***.

_____ 10. After Franny was attacked on the street and her pocketbook was stolen, she ***pulled herself together*** and went to the police.

C. Mrs. Black and Mrs. Brown are neighbors. Unfortunately, each of them learned that they have cancer. Their reactions, however, to this terrible news are different. Mrs. Black is very brave and controls her feelings, while Mrs. Brown is openly upset and unable to control her feelings. Using the expressions below, describe how each of them reacted. Use the past tense.

flip out	***pull oneself together***
not bat an eyelash	***fall apart***
come apart at the seams	***keep one's chin up***
go to pieces	***hold one's head up***
keep a stiff upper lip	

Mrs. Black	Mrs. Brown
She kept a stiff upper lip.	_____
_____	_____
_____	_____
_____	_____

(continued)

Mrs. Black	Mrs. Brown
_____	_____
_____	_____
_____	_____
_____	_____
_____	_____
_____	_____
_____	_____
_____	_____
_____	_____
_____	_____
_____	_____
_____	_____
_____	_____
_____	_____

COMMUNICATION   Read and discuss the following:

1. In what condition would a person be if somebody said, *"Pull yourself together"*?

2. In contrast to the attitude in this lesson, many psychologists say that in order to remain mentally healthy, we should express our emotions—that is, not hold them in. They therefore advise us to express how we feel. If, for example, we are sad, we should not try to hold back our tears. Do you agree with this advice? Why or why not?

3. Our body movements and the position of our body often communicate how we feel. Two of the expressions in this lesson, *hold one's head up* and *hold one's chin up*, refer to the position of the head when people are trying to control their emotions. What do these expressions indicate about the position of the head when someone is ashamed or sad?

4. The origin of the expression *be tough as nails* probably comes from the fact that nails are designed to resist bending. Nails, in other words, are strong. What do you suppose the origin of each of the following expressions is?

    keep a stiff upper lip   *come apart at the seams*

17
Thinking Ability

Have A lot on the ball

be out in left field
be out to lunch
be sharp as a tack
have a head on one's shoulders
have a lot on the ball
have a screw loose
not have anything between the ears

not know enough to come in out of the
 rain
not know whether one is coming or
 going
pick someone's brain
play with half a deck
put on one's thinking cap

SITUATION   Read the following dialog:

Sally, a university student, is coming out of class and sees her friend Bob.

Sally: Bob! Did you hear the news? My economics prof, Dr. Rosenfield, was nominated for the Nobel Prize.

Bob: That's great! I've heard that he's an expert in his field and that he really ***has a lot on the ball***.

Sally: Yes, he's very bright. Some call him the greatest economist of our times.

Bob: I sure wish I were in your class. My prof ***doesn't know whether he's coming or going***. He always seems confused and is never sure that what he says is right. Sometimes I think I know more about economics than he does.

Sally: Why don't you try to get into my section?

Bob: I already did. It's full.

ANALYSIS   Circle the best answer to the question below. Then turn the page and read the explanation for your choice. If you are wrong, choose again.

Why did Bob try to get into Dr. Rosenfield's class?

A.   He would like to be in the same class as Sally so he can see her more often.

B.   Bob recognizes that Dr. Rosenfield has one of the best minds in the field of economics.

C.   His own professor always arrives late and leaves early.

EXPLANATION A. Although Sally and Bob are friends, there is no indication that this is why Bob wanted to change classes.

B. Bob says that Dr. Rosenfield **has a lot on the ball**, meaning that Dr. Rosenfield is very smart. He would like to get into his class because he feels he would learn more. This is the best answer.

C. There is no reference in the conversation as to when Bob's professor arrives and leaves. If someone **does not know whether he is coming or going**, it means that the individual is not thinking clearly.

ATTITUDE   **Sally and Bob respect clear, rational thinking.**

EXPANSION A. Put a plus sign (+) in front of the expressions that illustrate clear thinking, and a minus sign (−) in front of those that do not show clear thinking.

_+_   Harry **has a lot on the ball**. He is very smart.

_____ 1. John **is sharp as a tack**. He graduated first in his class.

_____ 2. Mary **does not have anything between the ears**. She never understands anything.

_____ 3. Bill **is playing with half a deck**. He is really stupid.

_____ 4. Julie **has a head on her shoulders**. I always ask her for advice.

_____ 5. Larry **is out to lunch**. He does not know what is going on around him.

_____ 6. Sue **has a screw loose**. Everybody thinks her behavior is strange.

_____ 7. Greg **is out in left field**. He never knows the answers to the teacher's questions.

_____ 8. David **is putting on his thinking cap**. He is trying to find a solution to a problem.

_____ 9. Margaret **does not know enough to come in out of the rain**. She does not have any common sense.

_____ 10. Marianne **does not know whether she is coming or going**. She changes her mind every day.

_____ 11. Linda **is picking Dick's brain**. She wants to learn more about nuclear energy.

B. Larry Lawson is running for president of the freshman class at Midtown University. George and Karen, two of his classmates, disagree on his capabilities. George thinks Larry is very smart and would be a good class president. Karen thinks he is stupid and would be a poor choice. George and Karen are exchanging their points of view. Write "George" in front of the statement if it reflects George's opinion, and write "Karen" if it reflects her opinion.

Karen   "He **does not know whether he is coming or going**."

_____ 1. "He **is out to lunch**."

_____ 2. "He **has a screw loose**."

_____ 3. "He *is sharp as a tack*."

_____ 4. "He *has a head on his shoulders*."

_____ 5. "He *does not have anything between the ears*."

_____ 6. "He *does not know enough to come in out of the rain*."

_____ 7. "He *is playing with half a deck*."

_____ 8. "He *is out in left field*."

_____ 9. "He *has a lot on the ball*."

C. Using the idioms you have learned, write in the missing words. Put your answers in the present tense.

   Dick solves problems almost as fast as a computer. He *has a* lot *on the ball* .

1. Joanne will probably be president of the company one day. She _____ _____ ___ __ _____ tack .

2. Sharon asked Dick where the reverse gear on her bicycle was. She _____ _____ playing _____ _____ __ _____ .

3. Don had more job offers than anyone else in his class when he graduated. He _____ __ _____ ____ _____ _____ shoulders _____ .

4. Barb thinks Rome is the capital of France. She_____ _____ ____ _____ _____ field .

5. Harry cannot decide whether he wants to get married or not. One day he says yes, the next day he says no. He does not_____ whether _____ _____ ____ _____ ____ _____ .

6. Nick is trying to figure out what to buy his mother for her birthday. He is _____ ____ _____ thinking _____ _____ .

7. Ruth thinks 1 + 1 = 3. She does not _____ _____ _____ ____ _____ ears .

8. Jane did not understand the lecture, so she went to Richard's house for help. She wants to _____ Richard's brain _____ .

COMMUNICATION   Read and discuss the following:

1.   Students have to *put on their thinking caps* when they take exams. Teachers have to *put on their thinking caps* when they prepare lessons. Tell about times when you have to *put on your thinking cap*.

2.   If a person *is out in left field*, it means that the person does not know what is happening around him or her. This expression comes from the game of baseball. The player whose position is in left field is far from most of the action in the game. Try to guess what the original meanings of these expressions are.

      be out to lunch   have a screw loose

3.   People who *do not know whether they are coming or going* have trouble making decisions. An example of this might be a student who changes majors from one semester to the next. In one year this person goes from economics to political science to art. Tell about a time when you (or someone you know) *did not know whether you were coming or going*.

4.   People all over the world respect clear, rational thinking. However, people from different countries think in different ways. Describe something that people from countries other than your own do that you feel is irrational.

18
Privacy

Feel fenced in

be at someone's elbow
be pushy
breathe down someone's neck
breathing space
crash a party
elbow one's way in

elbow room
feel fenced in
feel hemmed in
keep someone at arm's length
move in on someone
tailgate

SITUATION Read the following dialog:

Ruth Peterson is an English teacher who likes to paint in her free time. She spent the entire afternoon in a local park painting. She is now at home with her roommate, Laurie, who is also an artist.

Laurie: It doesn't look as though you got very far with your painting today, Ruth.

Ruth: How could I? The park was full of kids and there was always someone **breathing down my neck**. They come right up beside me and watch what I'm doing. You know I can't work when that happens.

Laurie: It's the same with me. I can't paint either when someone **is at my elbow**, and you're right about the kids in the park. They surround you.

Ruth: It's too bad because the park could be such a nice place to work.

ANALYSIS Circle the best answer to the question below. Then turn the page and read the explanation for your choice. If you are wrong, choose again.

Why wasn't Ruth able to get much painting done?

A. She had to do lesson preparations for her English classes the next day.

B. She could not concentrate on her painting because the kids were standing right next to her.

C. Her neck hurt.

EXPLANATION   A.   Although most English teachers spend a lot of time preparing their lessons, we do not know when Ruth prepared hers—or even if she prepared hers at all.

B.   Ruth felt uncomfortable and had trouble painting because the children were standing too close to her. This is the best answer.

C.   The only reference to Ruth's neck was in the expression **breathe down someone's neck**, which means to follow every action closely.

ATTITUDE   **Ruth thinks of the area immediately around her as her own, and she does not like people to be in it.**

EXPANSION   A.   After reading the situations, decide whether you agree or disagree with the ending statements.

disagree   Dick is standing so close to Bruce that he **is breathing down his neck**. Bruce is probably going to ask Dick to move closer.

_____   1.   John's dormitory room is too small. He does not have enough **elbow room**. John is probably going to ask for a larger room.

_____   2.   Steve **feels fenced in**. He has to work because he has a wife and two children, but he does not like his job and he is looking for another one. Steve will probably quit his present job before finding a new one.

_____   3.   Gary likes Pat, Michael's girlfriend. Gary asked Pat to go to the movies, and Pat enjoyed his company so much that she decided to leave Michael. Gary **moved in on** Michael. Michael probably thanked Gary.

_____   4.   Jan **is pushy**. She is very aggressive and demands that things be done her way. Jan is probably very shy.

_____   5.   Margaret drives too closely behind other cars. It is dangerous to **tailgate** the way she does. People probably feel safe when they drive with Margaret.

_____   6.   Nancy, a college senior majoring in biology, admits that she does not like biology. She **feels hemmed in** because it is too late for her to change her major. Nancy will probably graduate with a degree in biology.

_____   7.   Paul gave a party but did not invite Kay and Bill. They came to the party anyway. She and Bill **crashed the party**. Paul was probably delighted that they came.

_____   8.   Ken shares a rather small office with two other people. They are always bumping into each other, and Ken feels that he does not have enough **breathing space**. Ken is probably glad when his co-workers are out of the office on business.

_____   9.   Dick likes Sally and is always asking her to go out to dinner with him. Sally, however, is not at all interested in Dick and she **keeps him at arm's length**. The next time Dick asks her out, Sally will probably refuse.

_____ 10. Sharon was standing in line at the movies when a woman stepped in front of her. The woman just **elbowed her way into** the line. Sally probably was happy to give her a place in the line.

_____ 11. Ann **is** always **at Bob's elbow**. He can never do anything alone because she is right there beside him. Ann probably likes Bob.

B. Answer the questions below with "yes" or "no."

no   Willy **is at John's elbow**. Is Willy far from John?

_____ 1. Howard **is pushy**. Is he likable?

_____ 2. Helen **feels fenced in**. Does she feel limited in what she can do?

_____ 3. Dan **keeps Dick at arm's length**. Does Dan like Dick?

_____ 4. Joann **moved in on** Barb. Was Barb happy with Joann?

_____ 5. Gail needs more **breathing space**. Should she move?

_____ 6. Polly **elbowed her way in**. Was she polite?

_____ 7. Jim **feels hemmed in**. Is he able to do what he wants to?

_____ 8. Larry **tailgates**. Is he a good driver?

_____ 9. Harold wants Joe to stop **breathing down his neck**. Is Joe too close?

_____ 10. Sally wants more **elbow room**. Does she feel crowded?

_____ 11. Joan **crashed the party**. Was the host angry with her?

C. Different people have different feelings about privacy. What bothers one person may not bother another. Using at least six expressions from the lesson, give a situation and then tell you how feel about it.

When I cook, I don't like other people to be in the kitchen. I need elbow room.

_____

_____

_____

_____

_____

_____

_____

_____

_____

_____

_____

_____

_____

_____

_____

_____

_____

_____

COMMUNICATION   Read and discuss the following:

1. A common expression in English is, "Two's company; three's a crowd." How can three people be a crowd?

2. When two people go into a dark movie theater, they try to stay close together so they won't lose each other. At what other times would you want someone to **be at your elbow**?

3. Approximately eighteen inches is the distance from others that most people in the United States feel comfortable with. There are different ways to refer to this, but one way is "The Great American Air Bubble." What is the acceptable distance between people in your country?

4. Imagine yourself in a park on a beautiful sunny day. There are three benches. On one bench are three people. The second bench is empty, and on the third there is one person. You want to sit down. Does it matter to you which bench you choose? Why?

19
Problem-Solving Ability

Take the bull by the horns

be off base
be right on target
beat around the bush
get down to the nuts and bolts
get to the heart of something
hem and haw

hit the bull's eye
hit the nail on the head
miss the mark
skirt the issue
take the bull by the horns
zero in on something

SITUATION   Read the following dialog:

Mr. O'Keefe, the president of a large automobile corporation, is consulting with two of his top executives, Ms. Francis and Mr. Siegel, who have researched the problem of low sales.

Mr. O'Keefe: I've read your reports and want to congratulate you on a thorough job. Have you anything further to add?

Ms. Francis: No, it's all there. As we've suspected all along, our biggest problem is that we're not meeting the demand for small cars.

Mr. Siegel: My findings are exactly the same. Ms. Francis **has hit the nail on the head**. With rising production and fuel costs, small cars will be the cars of the future.

Mr. O'Keefe: Good! Now is the time to **take the bull by the horns**. I'm convinced that we should increase our production of small cars immediately and hope that our sales will improve.

ANALYSIS   Circle the best answer to the question below. Then turn the page and read the explanation for your choice. If you are wrong, choose again.

Why is Mr. O'Keefe pleased about the findings of his colleagues?

A.   They were able to find a clear solution to the problem.

B.   He prefers to drive a small car.

C.   They agree with each other.

EXPLANATION   A.   Mr. O'Keefe was pleased that his colleagues had identified the cause of his company's problems. When he says it is time to **take the bull by the horns**, he means he is ready to take definite action to solve the problem. This is the best answer.

B.   From the conversation we do not know what size car Mr. O'Keefe drives.

C.   Although it is true that they all agree, and this might in fact please Mr. O'Keefe, he was particularly happy that Ms. Francis and Mr. Siegel were able to identify the company's problem.

ATTITUDE   **Mr. O'Keefe admires the ability to define a problem or situation directly and clearly.**

EXPANSION   A.   Place a plus sign (+) in front of the statements that show problem-solving ability, and a minus sign (−) in front of those that do not.

_+_   Someone who **takes the bull by the horns** meets problems directly regardless of any danger.

_____ 1.   Someone who **hems and haws** does not reply directly to a question.

_____ 2.   Someone who **is right on target** is absolutely correct.

_____ 3.   Someone who **beats around the bush** avoids giving a clear answer.

_____ 4.   Someone who **hits the bull's eye** is able to get something exactly right.

_____ 5.   Someone who **misses the mark** is not able to understand the most important thing.

_____ 6.   Someone who **zeroes in on** something discards what is unimportant and gets to the main problem.

_____ 7.   Someone who **skirts the issue** does not take a position on a point of discussion.

_____ 8.   Someone who **gets down to the nuts and bolts** works on the most important thing to talk about or know.

_____ 9.   Someone who **is off base** is not close to the answer.

_____ 10. Someone who **gets to the heart of** something understands the most important thing about it.

_____ 11. Someone who **hits the nail on the head** gets an answer exactly right.

B.   Peggy does not understand why she is having trouble saving money. Below is some information about each of her friends. Circle the names of the ones she would choose to help her.

(Ted) always **hits the nail on the head**.

1.   Mark always **skirts the issue**.
2.   Jan **is** usually **right on target**.
3.   Sarah easily **gets to the heart of** the matter.
4.   Sam often **misses the mark**.
5.   Chris often **hits the bull's eye**.

6. Dan *is* usually *off base*.

7. Karen *beats around the bush* a lot.

8. Lawrence *hems and haws*.

9. Cheri can *zero in on* a problem fast.

10. Marge always *takes the bull by the horns*.

11. Brian can *get down to the nuts and bolts of* any problem.

C. Ms. Francis is very good at solving problems, which is why Mr. O'Keefe went to her for help when car sales were low. Ms. Francis clearly defined the problem when she said that the company was not meeting the demand for small cars. Describe Ms. Francis in sentences of your own using all of the expressions from the following list. Some sentences will be in the negative.

be off base	*hit the bull's eye*
be right on target	*hit the nail on the head*
beat around the bush	*miss the mark*
get to the heart of (the matter, problem, etc.)	*skirt the issue*
	zero in on (the problem, etc.)
hem and haw	

Ms. Francis always hits the nail on the head.

_____

_____

_____

_____

_____

_____

_____

_____

_____

_____

_____

_____

_____

COMMUNICATION   Read and discuss the following:

1.   A friend of yours just changed hairstyles and has asked you if you like it. You do not. However, you do not want to hurt your friend by telling the truth, so you *skirt the issue*. How might you answer your friend?

2.   A successful doctor is one who is able to *zero in on* a patient's illness. Often, however, a successful lawyer is one who is able to *beat around the bush* in defending a client. Below is a list of other professional people. Separate them into those whose jobs require them to *zero in on* a problem and those whose jobs require them to *beat around the bush*. Support your answers.

detective	public relations director
politician	army general
teacher	diplomat
scientist	air traffic controller

3.   When people are not sure of what they want to say, they sometimes add meaningless sounds between words. The most common sounds in English are "umm" and "uh," as in "Umm . . . I . . . uh . . . am not sure that . . . uh . . . I agree with you." The expression *hem and haw*, meaning to avoid giving a clear answer, is an imitation of these sounds. What are some sounds (or words) that people use in your language when they *hem and haw*?

4.   At one time, people thought the sun revolved around the earth. They thought they *were right on target*, but were later proved to *be way off base*. Can you think of other examples?

20
Individual
Achievement

Be top dog

be in the big time
be low man on the totem pole
be the cream of the crop
be top dog
bring up the rear
feather in one's cap
get ahead

not hold a candle to
play second fiddle to someone
scrape the bottom of the barrel
sit up and take notice
steal the show
take one's hat off to someone
whip the pants off someone

SITUATION   Read the following dialog:

Today is the day Julie Burgess and her classmates have been waiting for. Several months ago, they took a national math exam. Today, in school, the results were announced. Julie is home now, telling her mother the news.

Julie: Hey, Mom. Remember that national math competition that everyone in our class entered? Well, Shirley won first prize!

Mrs. Burgess: She did? That's wonderful! She's a very capable young lady. She's sure to be a success and to **get ahead** in this world.

Julie: Yeah. Part of the prize is a $4,000 scholarship. She's really excited.

Mrs. Burgess: Well, she deserves to be proud. It's a **feather in her cap**. It would be nice to do something for her.

Julie: I already thought of that. A group of us are taking her out to dinner tomorrow.

ANALYSIS   Circle the best answer to the question below. Then turn the page and read the explanation for your choice. If you are wrong, choose again.

Why are Julie and Mrs. Burgess so happy for Shirley?

A.   She will not have to worry about paying for her college education.

B.   Shirley never did well in math before.

C.   They are pleased that she was honored.

81

EXPLANATION   A.   The $4000 scholarship will certainly help Shirley pay her college expenses, but this is not the main reason that Julie and Mrs. Burgess are happy for Shirley.

B.   If Shirley won first prize in a national competition, she is probably a very good math student.

C.   Julie and Mrs. Burgess are pleased that Shirley won national recognition. This is the best answer.

ATTITUDE   **Julie and Mrs. Burgess feel that individual achievement deserves recognition.**

EXPANSION   A.   Match the meaning of the idiom on the left with the definition on the right. There are two sections.

_e__ 1. No one even noticed the other actors. Steven Star **stole the show** from everyone else.

a. belonging to the best and most important group

_____ 2. Gail has seen almost every film in town. Tonight she is going to the only one she has not seen even though it is supposed to be bad. She is really **scraping the bottom of the barrel**.

b. be last

_____ 3. Sam, the star football player at a small college, just signed a contract to play with a national team. He **is in the big time** now.

c. act a smaller part; be less noticed

_____ 4. Mr. Johnson **is top dog** in the company. He is the president.

d. accept what is left after the best has been taken or done

_____ 5. Kathy is not quite as good as Jill in tennis. She **plays second fiddle to** Jill.

e. act so well that you get most of the attention

_____ 6. Tom was the worst. He **was low man on the totem pole**.

f. give honor, praise, or respect to

_____ 7. The president of the company **took his hat off to** the best employee. He complimented him on a job well done.

g. be the most important person

_____ 8. If Ed wants to **get ahead**, he has got to work hard.

h. the best of a group

_____ 9. John got the lowest mark in his class. He **brought up the rear**.

i. win by a large margin

_____ 10. Sally is always first in everything she does. She **is the cream of the crop**.

j. not be as good as

_____ 11. The basketball score was 150 to 38. Our team **whipped the pants off** the other team.

k. something to be proud of; an honor

_____ 12. When she started to sing, everyone **sat up and took notice** of her beautiful voice.

l. become successful

_____ 13. Sandy thinks modern literature does **not hold a candle to** the literature of the last century. She thinks nineteenth century literature is better.

m. do least well; do most poorly of a group

_____ 14. Winning the competition was another **feather in Mark's cap**.

n. be surprised and give attention to

B. Each year Mr. Reardon's company acknowledges outstanding performance with a dinner followed by a short ceremony where Mr. Reardon singles out the employees with the best sales records. Put a checkmark (✓) next to the comments that Mr. Reardon is likely to make.

✓ Mr. Prince's record is a **feather in his cap**.

_____ 1. Other departments **do not hold a candle to** ours.

_____ 2. Mr. Lowell **plays second fiddle to** Mrs. Hockett.

_____ 3. Ms. Hockett **is in the big time** now.

_____ 4. I **take my hat off to** Ms. Selleck.

_____ 5. I want you all to **sit up and take notice** of Ms. Black's performance.

_____ 6. Mr. Riley **is low man on the totem pole**.

_____ 7. Ms. Howell **is** really **getting ahead**.

_____ 8. Mr. Cromwell **brings up the rear**.

_____ 9. When I hired Mr. Richardson, I really **scraped the bottom of the barrel**.

_____ 10. Ms. Crowley **has stolen the show**.

_____ 11. Ms. Hickman **is the cream of the crop**.

_____ 12. Mr. Coe really **whipped the pants off** everyone else.

_____ 13. And finally, Mr. Morris **is top dog**.

C. Jeff Jergens, a sports announcer, is on the radio reporting about Killer Claw, the new boxing champion. Fill in the blanks with the missing words. Pay attention to tense.

Ladies and gentlemen, Killer Claw got another *feather* *in* *his*

___cap___ today. He really ___stole___ ___ ___ . Yes, that is right. The

new ___top___ ___ of the boxing world is Killer Claw. Killer started out as

___ ___man___ ___ ___ several years ago, and he

gradually ___got___ ___ . Until today he was never able to capture the

number one position. He ___played___ ___ ___ to

the old champ. Today's match had to be seen to be believed. After the first round,

he came alive and everyone immediately ___sat___ ___ ___ ___

___ . He ___ ___ ___pants___ ___ the old

champ. I ___ ___ ___ ___off___ to him.

COMMUNICATION   Read and discuss the following:

1.   In public schools, the end of the year may be marked by an awards ceremony where outstanding athletic or scholastic achievement is recognized. Do you have awards ceremonies in your country? Do you think they are a good idea? Why or why not?

2.   Many people feel that in order to **get ahead** and be a success in this world, they must have a good education. Do you agree? Why or why not?

3.   Talk about a situation like the one below that ends with the expression **not hold a candle to**.

Peggy and Martha both play the piano. Peggy can play very complicated musical pieces and she has performed for others. Martha, however, is just beginning to learn and can only play simple pieces. When it comes to playing the piano, Martha **does not hold a candle to** Peggy.

4.   Offer possible reasons why the following sentences might be said. For instance, if you see, "Patti **brought up the rear**," you might say, "She lost the race."

Max **is low man on the totem pole**.   Cindy **whipped the pants off** Carol.
Sheila **stole the show**.   Frank **is in the big time** now.

21
Speed/Efficiency

At a snail's pace

at a snail's pace
drag one's feet
get moving
get the ball rolling
get the show on the road
have lead in one's shoes
in a flash
in no time

in nothing flat
like a bat out of hell
quick as a wink
roll up one's sleeves
run around like a chicken with its
    head cut off
shake a leg

SITUATION Read the following dialog:

Pam Carpenter is on her lunch hour and has a big list of things she must do. She stops at Acme Pharmacy first.

Pam: I'd like this prescription filled, please. How long do you think it will take? I'm in a terrible hurry.

Pharmacist: I'll have it for you **in no time**.

                (two minutes later)

Pharmacist: Here you are. That'll be ten dollars.

Pam: That was fast. The pharmacist I went to last week really **dragged his feet**. I had to wait twenty minutes for him to fill this same prescription. You'll be seeing me again.

Pharmacist: I hope so. Have a nice day.

ANALYSIS Circle the best answer to the question below. Then turn the page and read the explanation for your choice. If you are wrong, choose again.

Why did Pam like the new pharmacist?

A.   He filled her prescription quickly.

B.   He was pleasant and friendly.

C.   The pharmacy was closer to where she works than the one she went to last week.

EXPLANATION   A.   The pharmacist said he would have the prescription ready ***in no time***, meaning very quickly, and he did. Pam was pleased that the pharmacist worked so quickly. This is the best answer.

B.   It is true that the pharmacist appeared pleasant and friendly, and although Pam probably appreciated this, she appreciated his speed and efficiency more.

C.   There is nothing in the conversation to indicate that the pharmacy was closer to work than the one she went to before.

ATTITUDE   **Pam puts a premium on doing things quickly and efficiently.**

EXPANSION   A.   Match the definition on the right with the idiomatic expression on the left. There are three sections.

___C___ 1. Mary started cooking dinner fifteen minutes ago and it is ready now. She did it ***in no time***.

a. very slow movement forward

_____ 2. Terry drove ***at a snail's pace***. All the cars on the road passed him.

b. start an activity

_____ 3. Let's ***get the show on the road***. We should have begun ten minutes ago.

c. in very little time

_____ 4. John said he would be back ***in a flash***. He left a minute ago. Here he comes now.

d. very quickly

_____ 5. Sam finished the race long before anyone else. He ran it ***in nothing flat***.

e. act slowly or reluctantly

_____ 6. John's mother told him to ***shake a leg*** because he was too slow. She wanted him to hurry up.

f. get started

_____ 7. Steve was ready to get the job done. He ***rolled up his sleeves*** and began.

g. be very active or busy, but with no direction or organization

_____ 8. Let's ***get moving***. We've waited long enough.

h. go faster

_____ 9. Nobody knew what they were doing. Everybody ***was running around like a chicken with its head cut off***.

i. prepare to work hard or seriously

_____ 10. It took Sally a half an hour to do a ten-minute job. She really ***dragged her feet***.

j. in very little time .

_____ 11. John came in last in the race. He must have **had lead in his shoes**.

k. going extremely quickly from one place to another

_____ 12. Everyone is afraid of that old house. The last person who went in came running out **like a bat out of hell**.

l. in very little time

_____ 13. Sue started her homework at 7:00 and finished fifteen minutes later. She did it **quick as a wink**.

m. start an activity or action

_____ 14. If we don't **get the ball rolling** soon, we won't have enough time to finish.

n. be slow in walking or movement

B. Read the following sentences and write either "agree" or "disagree" in front of each one.

disagree   If Mary did the job **in no time**, it took her hours to finish it.

_____ 1. If Mark's teacher told him to **shake a leg**, Mark probably was not working very fast.

_____ 2. If Bill **ran around like a chicken with its head cut off**, he probably had a very slow day.

_____ 3. If Kathy **rolled up her sleeves** and started to work, she was probably very lazy.

_____ 4. If Tom cooked dinner **quick as a wink**, he probably prepared something simple.

_____ 5. If Andy ran **like a bat out of hell**, he probably ran as fast as he could.

_____ 6. If Barb did her homework **in nothing flat**, she did not do it at all.

_____ 7. If Gene **has lead in his shoes**, he runs wherever he goes.

_____ 8. If Jake wanted to **get the ball rolling**, he was tired and wanted to go to bed.

_____ 9. If Dave came home **in a flash**, it probably took him hours to get home.

_____ 10. If Chris **is dragging her feet**, it will probably take her a while to get where she is going.

_____ 11. If Ann walked **at a snail's pace**, she was not in a hurry.

_____ 12. If Karen told her roommate to **get moving**, she was afraid they would be late.

_____ 13. If Lynn wanted to **get the show on the road**, she probably took a nap.

C. Fill in the blanks with the appropriate expression from this lesson.

One day last week, Gene and Ken went to a rock concert. They left late because

Ken *dragged his* _____ feet _____ even though Gene kept telling him to

_____ __ __leg__ . It seemed to Gene that Ken ____had____ _____ ____

_____ ____shoes____ , and Gene wanted to _____ _____ __show__ ____

_____ _____ . When they finally left, Gene drove _____ __ __bat__

_____ ____ _____ in order to get there on time. While Gene parked the

car, Ken got the tickets. Ken said he would be back ____quick____ ____ __

_____ , but it took him a lot longer than he thought it would. He said there

was a huge crowd in front of the ticket office and that everyone was

____running____ _____ _____ __ __chicken__ _____

_____ _____ _____ _____ . After they got to their seats, they learned

that the concert would not start on time. They were angry and wished the rock

group would ____get____ _____ _____ _____rolling_____ . Gene and Ken

knew they would get home late because traffic would be bad and they would

have to drive ____ __ _____ __pace__ .

COMMUNICATION   Read and discuss the following:

1.   There are several expressions in English that are used to suggest that people should begin an activity. Some of these expressions are:

   Shake a leg!   **Let's get the show on the road.**
   Let's get the ball rolling.   **Let's roll up our sleeves and get to work.**
   Let's get moving.

   Make up a short exchange like the following that ends with one of the above expressions.

   Mary and Frank are getting ready to go to their friends' house, the Shepherd's, for dinner.

   Mary: Frank, what's taking you so long? We told the Shepherds we'd be there at seven.

   Frank: I'll be ready in a minute. I just have to put my tie on.

   Mary: Well, hurry up. Let's **get the show on the road**.

2.   A well-known proverb in English, "Haste makes waste," means that if people work too quickly, they will make mistakes. Discuss the possibility that speed can result in inefficiency rather than efficiency.

3.   Fast-food restaurants, which often serve hamburgers and chicken, are based on speed and efficiency. Why would a person choose to eat in a fast-food restaurant instead of a traditional restaurant?

4.   When someone **runs around like a chicken with its head cut off**, that person is very active or busy, but with no direction or organization. What do you suppose the origin of this expression is?

22
Kindness/Aid

Bend over backward for someone

be hard-hearted
be tight-fisted
be warm-hearted
bend over backward for someone
cut someone to the quick
do the footwork
give someone the shirt off one's back
go out of one's way for someone

go to bat for someone
have a heart
have a heart of gold
have a heart of stone
heart goes out to someone
heart is in the right place
lend someone an ear

SITUATION Read the following dialog:

Emily and Karen are sharing a room in a local hospital. They have each had a minor operation, but they are feeling fine now and are ready to go home. They are talking about their nurses.

Emily: How about buying a little gift for Miss Hallen, our day nurse? She was so good to us, and did far more than was necessary.

Karen: A great idea. And you're right. She'd do anything for you. She **would give you the shirt off her back**. I'm afraid I can't say the same for our night nurse, though. Old Mrs. Black wasn't too friendly.

Emily: I'll say. What a mean, **hard-hearted** person. I wonder why she decided to be a nurse?

Karen: Who knows? At least we were lucky with one of them. Maybe we can find something for Miss Hallen in the hospital gift shop on the first floor.

Emily: Okay. Let's go down now.

ANALYSIS Circle the best answer to the question below. Then turn the page and read the explanation for your choice. If you are wrong, choose again.

Why are Emily and Karen going to buy a gift for their day nurse, Miss Hallen, and not for their night nurse, Mrs. Black?

A. They know Miss Hallen better than Mrs. Black.

B. Miss Hallen was very nice to them, and did extra things for them.

C. They want to make Mrs. Black jealous.

EXPLANATION   A.   Because Miss Hallen took care of them during the day, they might know her better than Mrs. Black, but this is not why they decided to buy her a gift.

B.   They want to show Miss Hallen that they appreciate her kindness. This is the best answer.

C.   Mrs. Black will probably never know that Emily and Karen gave a gift to Miss Hallen and not to her. Although the women did not like Mrs. Black, there is no indication that they wanted to make her jealous.

ATTITUDE   **Emily and Karen appreciate help and kindness.**

EXPANSION   A.   Put a plus sign (+) in front of those sentences that show kindness or aid, and a minus sign (−) in front of those that do not.

_+_   Someone who would **give another the shirt off his back** is extremely generous.

_____   1.   Someone who **cuts another to the quick** hurts that person's feelings deeply.

_____   2.   Someone who **does the footwork** for another carries out that person's plans, often attending to details.

_____   3.   Someone who **bends over backward for** another makes a great effort for that person.

_____   4.   Some who **is hard-hearted** is unfeeling.

_____   5.   Someone who **goes to bat for** another helps that person in time of trouble or need.

_____   6.   Someone who **goes out his way for** another makes an extra effort and does more than usual.

_____   7.   Someone who **has a heart** is generous and sympathetic.

_____   8.   Someone whose **heart goes out to** another feels very sorry for that person.

_____   9.   Someone whose **heart is in the right place** has good intentions.

_____   10.   Someone who **has a heart of gold** is generous and giving.

_____   11.   Someone who **has a heart of stone** is pitiless and unfeeling.

_____   12.   Someone who **lends another an ear** listens to that person.

_____   13.   Someone who **is tight-fisted** is reluctant to give or spend money.

_____   14.   Someone who **is warm-hearted** is loving and considerate.

B.   If you had a problem or needed help, which of the following people would you go to? Indicate your answer by circling the names.

(George) would **give you the shirt off his back**.

1.   Mark would **bend over backward for** you.

2.   Tom **has a heart of stone**.

3.   Bob's **heart is in the right place.**

4. Sharon will *lend you an ear*.
5. Sue can *cut you to the quick*.
6. Margaret *will go to bat for* you.
7. Jim *has a heart of gold*.
8. Bill is *hard-hearted*.
9. Karen's *heart goes out to* anyone in trouble.
10. Gene would *go out of his way* to help his friends.
11. Frank *is tight-fisted*.
12. Paula *is warm-hearted*.
13. Linda does not mind *doing the footwork*.
14. Joe *has a heart*.

C. A eulogy is a public speech in which only good things are said about someone who has recently died. Using all of the idioms in the list below, finish writing this eulogy. Be sure to use the past tense.

be warm-hearted   *go to bat for someone*
bend over backward for someone   *have a heart of gold*
give someone the shirt off one's back   *heart is in the right place*
go out of one's way for someone

Dear friends and loved ones. We are gathered here today in remembrance of John Doe, a man who was loved by us all.

To anyone in need, he would have given the shirt off his back.

_____

_____

_____

_____

_____

_____

_____

_____

_____

_____

_____

COMMUNICATION   Read and discuss the following:

1. Truman Capote, a twentieth-century American author, wrote a nonfiction novel about two men who had been sentenced to death for killing a family of four for no apparent reason. He called his novel *In Cold Blood*. What do you suppose the title means, and why do you suppose he chose it?

2. Have you ever ***done the footwork*** for somebody, or asked someone to ***do the footwork*** for you? Explain.

3. Describe a situation in which you might say, "My ***heart goes out to*** you."

4. As illustrated by several of the expressions in this lesson, the heart is often associated with kindness or the lack of it. Why do you suppose kindness is associated with the heart and not with some other part of the body?

Let off steam

23
Control of Anger

be fit to be tied	*grit one's teeth*
be hot and bothered	*hold one's temper*
be hot under the collar	*keep a civil tongue*
be hot-headed	*let off steam*
blow up	*make someone's blood boil*
count to ten	*reach the boiling point*
fly off the handle	*see red*
give someone a piece of one's mind	

SITUATION   Read the following dialog:

Sandy is talking to her roommate, Karen.

Sandy: Do you know what Mary did?

Karen: No. What?

Sandy: I lent her my history notes because she lost hers, and then she lost mine. We have a big exam tomorrow, and I don't know what I'm going to do. I feel like calling her up and telling her how angry I am.

Karen: Wait! You'd better **count to ten** before you do. Give yourself a chance to calm down. Mary's a good friend of yours, and if you do that, she might never speak to you again.

Sandy: I suppose I'll be all right after a while, but right now I'm so mad I **see red**.

Karen: Why don't you go for a walk before you call her?

Sandy: That's probably not a bad idea.

ANALYSIS   Circle the best answer to the question below. Then turn the page and read the explanation for your choice. If you are wrong, choose again.

Why did Karen suggest that Sandy wait a while before calling Mary?

A.   Sandy was so angry that she might say something she would later regret.

B.   Karen thought that Mary was in history class, and not at home.

C.   Karen likes Mary and does not want Sandy to say unkind things to her.

EXPLANATION   A.   Karen thought that Sandy should calm down before calling Mary so she would not damage their friendship. This is the best answer.

B.   Sandy and Mary are taking the same history class. If Mary were in class, Sandy probably would be too.

C.   Although Karen probably does like Mary and does not want Sandy to say ugly things to her, Karen's main concern is that because Sandy is angry, she will say things that she will later regret.

ATTITUDE   **Karen feels that people should control their anger.**

EXPANSION   A.   Everybody wanted to give a graduation party. Paul, however, insisted that he have the party at his house, and he would not let anyone help him. He said he wanted to surprise them with something special. Finally his friends agreed and let him organize it alone. The day of the party, however, he announced that he had prepared nothing, and did not want to give the party. It was too late for anybody else to organize one. Below is how they reacted. Put a plus sign (+) for those who controlled their anger, and a minus sign (−) for those who did not.

_−_   When Betty heard the news, she **saw red**. She said she would never speak to Paul again.

_____   1.   Stanley **reached the boiling point**. He slammed the door in Paul's face.

_____   2.   Pat **flew off the handle**. She actually hit Paul. She had really been looking forward to the party, and she was very disappointed.

_____   3.   Greg **kept a civil tongue**. He telephoned Paul and asked him as calmly as he could why he had prepared nothing.

_____   4.   Tom **let off steam**. He telephoned Patti and told her what he thought of Paul.

_____   5.   Cindy **blew up**. She called Paul all sorts of names.

_____   6.   It **made Jack's blood boil**. He got into a fight with Paul.

_____   7.   Linda **gave Paul a piece of her mind**. She told him he was immature, irresponsible, and undependable.

_____   8.   Carl **grit his teeth**. When he saw Paul, he tried to be friendly.

_____   9.   Dave **was fit to be tied**. He had wanted to have the party at his house, and he would have given a good one. Now it was too late to do anything.

_____   10.   Becky **held her temper**. The others could not understand why she did not tell Paul what she thought of him.

_____   11.   Helen, who **is hot-headed** anyway, told Paul she never wanted to see him again.

_____   12.   Nick **was hot under the collar**. He did not have one kind word to say about Paul.

_____   13.   When Margie saw Paul, she **counted to ten**. Afterwards, she was not quite so angry.

_____   14.   Sarah **was hot and bothered**. She hung up on Paul when he called her.

B. It is very difficult to work with Stanley because he gets angry very easily. He is, however, working on controlling his anger. Sometimes he is successful, and sometimes he is not. Write "yes" if he was able to control his anger, and "no" if he was not.

no   When talking with Tim, Stanley **saw red**.

_____ 1. With Barb, Stanley **was fit to be tied**.

_____ 2. When talking with Denise, Stanley **blew up**.

_____ 3. When he was with Carol, Stanley **was hot-headed**.

_____ 4. When talking with Lawrence, Stanley **held his temper**.

_____ 5. When Stanley saw Al, he **gave him a piece of his mind**.

_____ 6. When talking with Peter, Stanley **reached the boiling point**.

_____ 7. When Emily called, Stanley **was hot under the collar**.

_____ 8. With Karen, Stanley **kept a civil tongue**.

_____ 9. When Stanley saw Tom, he **let off steam**.

_____ 10. With Priscilla, Stanley **grit his teeth**.

_____ 11. When talking with Patrick, Stanley **flew off the handle**.

_____ 12. When Stanley saw Sam, he **counted to ten**.

_____ 13. When Stanley saw Bill, it **made his blood boil**.

_____ 14. With Ed, Stanley **was hot and bothered**.

C. Suppose that you were in Paul's graduating class, and like most of his classmates, you were openly very angry with him. Using the expressions below, describe how you reacted when Paul said he was not going to have the party. Use the past tense.

see red	*give someone a piece of one's mind*
blow up	*be hot under the collar*
reach the boiling point	*let off steam*
be fit to be tied	*make someone's blood boil*
fly off the handle	

I saw red. _____

_____

_____

_____

_____

_____

_____

_____

_____

_____

_____

_____

_____

_____

_____

_____

_____

_____

_____

COMMUNICATION   Read and discuss the following:

1. Many of the expressions referring to anger deal with heat, such as **be hot and bothered**, **be hot-headed**, and **be hot under the collar**. Others refer to boiling, such as **reach the boiling point** and **make someone's blood boil**. What connection do you see between heat and anger?

2. In the United States, red is the color that is associated with anger. When people **see red**, they are angry. What color is associated with anger in your country?

3. Everybody gets angry occasionally. First, think of a time when you **flew off the handle**; then, think of a time when you **held your temper**.

4. Do you find that when you are angry, if you **count to ten**—that is, wait a while before acting on your anger—that your anger lessens? If so, do you think this is a good way to deal with anger?

24 Harmony

Let sleeping dogs lie

bury the hatchet
button one's lips
flow with the tide
get off someone's back
handle someone with kid gloves
hold one's tongue
iron things out
jump down someone's throat
kick up a fuss
let sleeping dogs lie

let well enough alone
make waves
mind one's own business
open a can of worms
rock the boat
see eye to eye
throw a monkey wrench into something
upset the applecart

SITUATION   Read the following dialog:

Harold and Maude, a retired couple, are talking about their daughter, Peg, and their grandson, Timmy, who is three years old.

Maude: You know, I'm slightly annoyed with Peg. This is the third time this week she's asked me to take care of Timmy while she goes shopping. I wonder if I should tell her how I feel?

Harold: Aw, honey, why **make waves**? You don't want to upset Peg, do you? You know you enjoy Timmy as much as I do.

Maude: Yes, of course I do. I love having him here. It's just that I don't think Peg should take advantage of us. Why shouldn't I say something to her?

Harold: Don't **upset the applecart**, Maude. We're lucky that we get along so well with Peg and her husband. We certainly don't want to do anything that would change that. Besides, I think it's nice that Peg feels free to call on us when she needs us.

Maude: I guess you're right, Harold. I won't say anything to her.

ANALYSIS   Circle the best answer to the question below. Then turn the page and read the explanation for your choice. If you are wrong, choose again.

Why does Harold feel that Maude should not speak to Peg about how she feels?

A.   He does not want Maude to do anything that would hurt the relationship they have with their daughter.

B.   He is afraid they will never see their grandson again.

C.   He is never home when Timmy is there, so he is not affected.

97

EXPLANATION A. Harold is encouraging his wife not to do anything that would upset the good relationship they have with their daughter. This is the best answer.

                B. It is unlikely that if Maude spoke to Peg about being taken advantage of, Peg would stop visiting her parents.

                C. We know that Harold is often home when Timmy is there because he talked about enjoying Timmy's visits.

ATTITUDE **Harold feels that there are times when people should not do anything that would upset others or strain relationships.**

EXPANSION A. Match the definition on the right with the idiomatic expression on the left. There are three sections.

_f_ 1. Sally planned a surprise party for Bill, but Margaret accidentally **upset the applecart** by telling him.	a. do something that causes a plan that is going smoothly to be changed
____ 2. George and Karen have been arguing all day. It all started when George **jumped down Karen's throat** for burning the breakfast.	b. agree
____ 3. It is a good thing Jim **held his tongue**. If he had talked back, the police officer might have given him a ticket.	c. not interfere with what someone else is doing.
____ 4. Paul and his wife **see eye to eye**. Whatever Paul wants to do, his wife does too.	d. suddenly become very angry at somebody
____ 5. The preparations for the trip had been going smoothly and everyone was all ready, but Mark **threw a monkey wrench into** things by being late.	e. be silent
____ 6. Jan told Steve to **mind his own business**. He had been telling her how to do her job and she did not want his help.	f. ruin something, often by surprise or accident

_____ 7. Everyone had agreed to spend the day at the beach. Then John changed his mind and said he wanted to go to the mountains. John **rocked the boat**.

_____ 8. Sam and Bill finally **buried the hatchet**. After fighting for weeks, they agreed to stop.

_____ 9. Mary told Sue to **get off her back**. Mary was very busy and Sue would not leave her alone.

_____ 10. Bill did not like what his friends had decided to do, but he went along with it anyway. He **flowed with the tide**.

_____ 11. Steve **kicked up** such **a fuss** at the restaurant that the management asked him to leave.

_____ 12. Sally's teacher told her to **button her lip**. She was so noisy that she was disturbing the class.

g. stop bothering someone

h. accept what goes on; not object

i. make trouble; make a disturbance

j. stop talking

k. do something that may upset a plan

l. make peace

- - - - - - - - - -

_____ 13. Joe and Mike had been arguing with each other all day. Finally, their boss told them to stop fighting and **iron things out**.

_____ 14. Barb did not tell her mother that she had broken her mother's favorite vase. Instead, she bought a new one. She thought it was better to **let sleeping dogs lie**.

_____ 15. Dick does not get along well with others at work. He is always trying to **make waves**.

_____ 16. Linda gets depressed easily so her teacher treats her very carefully. He **handles her with kid gloves**.

_____ 17. Gene does not like to discuss politics. Every time he **opens that can of worms**, he gets into an argument.

_____ 18. Dave was not satisfied that Tom admitted he was wrong. He also wanted an apology and a promise from Tom that he would never do it again. Tom refused. Dave should have **let well enough alone**.

m. raise a complex problem or complicated situation

n. be very gentle

o. not anger someone if it can be avoided

p. reach an agreement about a difference

q. be happy with what is good enough, because asking for more might cause trouble

r. create a disturbance

B. Becky and Ruth are roommates who try to get along with each other in spite of their differences. Below is a day by day account of how well they succeeded in keeping a harmonious relationship. Make two lists—one of the times when they got along, and another of the times when they had differences.

Monday morning, Becky **made waves**.

1. Monday afternoon, Becky and Ruth **ironed things out**.
2. Tuesday morning Ruth **jumped down Becky's throat**.
3. Tuesday afternoon, Becky told Ruth to **get off her back**.
4. Tuesday night, Becky and Ruth **buried the hatchet**.
5. Wednesday morning, Becky and Ruth decided to **let sleeping dogs lie**.
6. Wednesday afternoon, Becky **threw a monkey wrench into** things.
7. Thursday morning, Ruth told Becky to **mind her own business**.
8. Thursday afternoon, Becky **held her tongue**.
9. Thursday night, Becky and Ruth **flowed with the tide**.
10. Friday morning, Ruth **opened a can of worms**.
11. Friday afternoon, Becky **buttoned her lip**.
12. Saturday morning, Becky **upset the applecart**.
13. Saturday afternoon, Ruth **handled Becky with kid gloves**.
14. Saturday night, Ruth **kicked up a fuss**.
15. Sunday morning, Ruth and Becky **let well enough alone**.
16. Sunday afternoon, Becky **rocked the boat**.
17. Finally, Sunday night, Ruth and Becky **saw eye to eye**.

Times when Becky and Ruth got along	Times when Becky and Ruth had differences
	Monday morning.

C. The following item recently appeared in a local newspaper:

On Monday night at 9:00, a fight broke out between a husband and wife in a fashionable restaurant downtown. According to witnesses, the couple began to argue shortly after finishing dinner. A waiter, who wishes to remain unidentified, said the argument started when the husband compared the restaurant's cooking to his wife's. Damage to the restaurant was estimated at $500. The husband was treated for minor injuries.

Using all of the idioms from the following list, make sentences beginning with:

None of this would have happened if the husband had (hadn't) . . .
None of this would have happened if the wife had (hadn't) . . .

button one's lips	*jump down someone's throat*
bury the hatchet	*open a can of worms*
flow with the tide	*rock the boat*
handle someone with kid gloves	*see eye to eye*
hold one's tongue	*throw a monkey wrench into something*
iron things out	*upset the applecart*

None of this would have happened if the husband hadn't made waves.

_____

_____

_____

_____

_____

_____

_____

_____

_____

_____

COMMUNICATION Read and discuss the following:

1. A hatchet, a hand tool used today for cutting wood, was the North American Indians' traditional weapon of war. To declare peace, the Indians would sometimes throw the hatchet into the ground. This is the origin of the expression ***bury the hatchet***. Ways of declaring peace are not the same throughout the world. Do you know of any traditional methods of declaring peace? How is it commonly done today?

2. Can you think of a time when you ***jumped down someone's throat***, and then regretted it?

3. Think of a time when you and someone else tried to ***iron things out***.

4. Suppose that a friend of yours who is out of town has lent you his car. You are in a minor accident, and there is some damage to the rear of his car. You have it repaired, and nobody can tell there was ever any damage. When your friend returns, what do you do? Do you tell him about the accident and risk ***making waves*** because you know he will be upset, or do you ***hold your tongue*** and not tell him about the accident in order not to upset him? Explain your answer.

Answer Key
for Expansion Exercises A and B

1 PERSEVERANCE

A   1. ✓   B.   Sentences to be crossed out:
    2.   1. She puts on her coat to leave.
    3. ✓   2. Yes, he did.
    4. ✓   3. George would make a good leader.
                4. She told him that if he does not want to go, he should not.

2 RESPONSIBILITY

A.	Group A	Group B	B.	
	Pat	Polly		1. −
	Mary	Jack		2. −
		Jill		3. −
		Paul		4. +
		Mark		5. −
				6. +

3 EASE OF EFFORT

A.   1. ✓
    2.
    3.
    4. ✓
    5. ✓
    6. ✓
    7. ✓

B.   Sentences to be crossed out:
1. She got the lowest mark in the class.
2. Another night, he carried a tray of eggs home from the store without breaking any.
3. He will always have to worry about money.
4. Everyone wants to dance with him.
5. Not too long ago, she was in a restaurant at a table next to her favorite film star.
6. It only took him seven years to learn Portuguese.
7. Phil never catches anything.

4 HARD WORK

A.		B.	
1. Carl		1. C	
2. Eric		2. C	
3. Carl		3. A	
4. Eric		4. B	
5. Carl		5. C	
6. Carl		6. A	
7. Carl		7. B	

5 COMPROMISE

A.		
1. yes	4. no	
2. no	5. yes	
3. yes	6. yes	

B.   *Areas in which Mr. O'Leary is willing to compromise*   *Areas in which Mr. O'Leary is unwilling to compromise*

Willing to compromise	Unwilling to compromise
tax reform	health care
foreign policy	capital punishment
welfare	
anti-pollution	
law and order	

6 INDEPENDENCE

A.		
1. I	5. I	
2. D	6. D	
3. D	7. D	
4. D	8. I	

B.   Sentences to be crossed out:
Be a yes-man.
Always remember to *be led by the nose.*

7 HONESTY/DIRECTNESS

A. 1. yes   B. 1. Mark
   2. no   2. Mark
   3. yes   3. Mark
   4. yes   4. Mark
   5. yes   5. Mark
   6. no   6. Walter
   7. yes   7. Mark
   8. yes   8. Walter

8 FAIR PLAY

A. 1. b   B. 1. no
   2. a   2. yes
   3. b   3. no
   4. a   4. no
   5. a   5. yes
   6. b   6. no
   7. b   7. yes
   8. a   8. yes

9 EXPERIENCE

A. 1. −   5. +
   2. +   6. −
   3. +   7. −
   4. +   8. +

B. Part of the sentence to be crossed out:
   1. He always gets lost going there,
   2. and she does not know anything.
   3. She is very naive
   4. and he understands all the rules.
   5. This is the first time she has painted a room,
   6. but she will probably make the same mistake next time.
   7. and he has performed hundreds of operations.
   8. and he has done it a thousand times before.

10 COOPERATION

A. 1. individual   6. group
   2. group   7. group
   3. individual   8. individual
   4. group   9. group
   5. group

B. 1. George   6. (Sue)
   2. (Mary)   7. Jim
   3. (Karen)   8. (Bill)
   4. Paul   9. (Sally)
   5. (Tom)

11 IMPROBABILITY OF DESIRED OUTCOME

A. 1. no   6. yes   B. 1. A   6. B
   2. yes   7. no   2. B   7. A
   3. yes   8. yes   3. B   8. B
   4. no   9. no   4. A   9. A
   5. no   5. B

12 FRIENDLINESS

A. 1. no   6. yes
    2. no   7. no
    3. yes   8. no
    4. no   9. no
    5. no

B. 1. J~~oh~~n   6. M~~ar~~k

    2. M~~ar~~y   7. Sa~~n~~dy

    3. (Jim)   8. (Barb)

    4. (Karen)   9. (Lesley)

    5. Ma~~r~~garet

13 HAPPINESS

A. 1. −   6. +   B. 1. u   6. h
    2. +   7. +   2. h   7. u
    3. +   8. −   3. u   8. u
    4. −   9. −   4. u   9. h
    5. −   10. +   5. h   10. h

14 LIMITATIONS

A. 1. A   6. A   B. 1. A   5. A
    2. B   7. A   2. A   6. B
    3. B   8. B   3. B   7. A
    4. A   9. B   4. B   8. B
    5. B   10. A

15 HUMILITY

A. 1. likely   6. likely   B. 1. yes   6. yes
    2. unlikely   7. unlikely   2. no   7. no
    3. unlikely   8. likely   3. yes   8. yes
    4. unlikely   9. unlikely   4. no   9. yes
    5. likely   10. likely   5. yes   10. yes

16 CONTROL OF EMOTIONS

A. 1. +   7. +   B. 1. yes   6. yes
    2. −   8. +   2. no   7. yes
    3. +   9. −   3. yes   8. no
    4. +   10. +   4. no   9. no
    5. −   11. −   5. yes   10. yes
    6. +

17 THINKING ABILITY

A. 1. +   7. −   B. 1. Karen   6. Karen
    2. −   8. +   2. Karen   7. Karen
    3. −   9. −   3. George   8. Karen
    4. +   10. −   4. George   9. George
    5. −   11. +   5. Karen
    6. −

18 PRIVACY

A. 1. agree   7. disagree   B. 1. no   7. no
    2. disagree   8. agree   2. yes   8. no
    3. disagree   9. agree   3. no   9. yes
    4. disagree   10. disagree   4. no   10. yes
    5. disagree   11. agree   5. yes   11. yes
    6. agree   6. no

19 PROBLEM-SOLVING ABILITY

A. 1. −   7. −
    2. +   8. +
    3. −   9. −
    4. +   10. +
    5. −   11. +
    6. +

B. 1. Mark   7. Karen

    2. (Jan)   8. Lawrence

    3. (Sarah)   9. (Cheri)

    4. Sam   10. (Marge)

    5. (Chris)   11. (Brian)

    6. Dan

20 INDIVIDUAL ACHIEVEMENT

A. 1. e   8. l   B. 1. ✓   8.
    2. d   9. m   2.   9.
    3. a   10. h   3. ✓   10. ✓
    4. g   11. i   4. ✓   11. ✓
    5. c   12. n   5. ✓   12. ✓
    6. b   13. j   6.   13. ✓
    7. f   14. k   7. ✓

21 SPEED/EFFICIENCY

A. 1. c   5. j   11. n   B. 1. agree   6. disagree   10. agree
    2. a   6. h   12. k   2. disagree   7. disagree   11. agree
    3. b   7. i   13. l   3. disagree   8. disagree   12. agree
    4. d   8. f   14. m   4. agree   9. disagree   13. disagree
           9. g   5. agree
           10. e

22 KINDNESS/AID

A. 1. −   8. +
    2. +   9. +
    3. +   10. +
    4. −   11. −
    5. +   12. +
    6. +   13. −
    7. +   14. +

B. 1. Mark   8. Bill

2. Tom   9. Karen

3. Bob   10. Gene

4. Sharon   11. Frank

5. Sue   12. Paula

6. Margaret   13. Linda

7. Jim   14. Joe

23 CONTROL OF ANGER

A. 1. −   8. +   B. 1. no   8. yes
    2. −   9. −   2. no   9. no
    3. +   10. +   3. no   10. yes
    4. −   11. −   4. yes 11. no
    5. −   12. −   5. no   12. yes
    6. −   13. +   6. no   13. no
    7. −   14. −   7. no   14. no

24 HARMONY

A. 1. f   7. k   13. p
    2. d   8. l   14. o
    3. e   9. g   15. r
    4. b   10. h   16. n
    5. a   11. i   17. m
    6. c   12. j   18. q

B. *Times when Becky and Ruth got along*   *Times when Becky and Ruth had differences*
    Monday afternoon   Monday morning
    Tuesday night   Tuesday morning
    Wednesday morning   Tuesday afternoon
    Thursday afternoon   Wednesday afternoon
    Thursday night   Thursday morning
    Friday afternoon   Friday morning
    Saturday afternoon   Saturday morning
    Sunday morning   Saturday night
    Sunday night   Sunday afternoon

Glossary

add insult to injury hurt someone's feelings after doing that person harm; make bad trouble worse (Fair Play)

all or nothing unwilling to compromise (Compromise)

at a snail's pace very slow movement forward (Speed/Efficiency)

bare one's soul tell everything (Honesty/Directness)

be a breeze be very easy (Ease of Effort)

be a copycat imitate someone (Independence)

be a good sport be someone who has a good sense of fair play (Fair Play)

be a hit below the belt be an unfair or cowardly act; do something that is against the rules of sportsmanship or justice (Fair Play)

be a loner avoid the company of others (Cooperation)

be a long shot be a risk that has little chance of success (Improbability of Desired Outcome)

be a mama's boy be overly dependent on one's mother (Independence)

be a yes-man try to be liked by agreeing with everyone (Independence)

be all thumbs be awkward, especially with hands; be clumsy (Ease of Effort)

be an old hand at something have lots of experience (Experience)

be at someone's elbow be very close (Privacy)

be cool as a cucumber be very calm and brave (Control of Emotions)

be cool toward someone be unfriendly toward someone (Friendliness)

be down in the dumps be depressed (Happiness)

be down to earth be very natural (Humility)

be easy as pie be very easy (Ease of Effort)

be fit to be tied be very angry or upset (Control of Anger)

be green lack training, experience or conditioning (Experience)

be hard-hearted be unfeeling, unmerciful (Kindness/Aid)

be hot and bothered be excited and angry (Control of Anger)

be hot under the collar be angry (Control of Anger)

be hot-headed be easily angered (Control of Anger)

be in seventh heaven be extremely happy (Happiness)

be in the big time belong to the top group; be in the leading class (Individual Achievement)

be like looking for a needle in a haystack be like looking for something that will be very difficult to find (Improbability of Desired Outcome)

be low man on the totem pole be last (Individual Achievement)

be off-base not agree with fact; be wrong (Problem-Solving Ability)

be on cloud nine be extremely happy (Happiness)

be on one's own live independently of others; work without help or guidance (Independence)

be on top of the world feel extremely good (Happiness)

be out in left field be far from the right answer (Thinking Ability)

be out of one's hands not be under one's control (Improbability of Desired Outcome)

be out of sorts be in a bad temper (Happiness)

be out to lunch be inattentive; daydream; be stupid (Thinking Ability)

be pushy be aggressive (Privacy)

be right on target get something exactly right (Problem-Solving Ability)

be sharp as a tack be smart, very bright (Thinking Ability)

be the cream of the crop be the best; be the top choice (Individual Achievement)

be tickled pink be very happy (Happiness)

be tied to one's mother's apron strings be overly dependent on one's mother (Independence)

be tight-fisted be reluctant to give or spend money (Kindness/Aid)

be too big for one's breeches be too sure of one's own importance (Humility)

be top dog be the most important person (Individual Achievement)

be tough as nails be able to endure a lot (Control of Emotions)

be tough-skinned   be able to endure a lot (Control of Emotions)
be two-faced   be hypocritical (Honesty/Directness)
be up front   be totally honest (Honesty/Directness)
be warm-hearted   have sympathy or affection (Kindness/Aid)
be wet behind the ears   be inexperienced; not know how to do something (Experience)
beat around the bush   talk about things without giving a clear answer; avoid the question or point (Problem-Solving Ability)
beat the odds   win although one is at a disadvantage (Improbability of Desired Outcome)
bend over backward for someone   make a great effort; try very hard (Kindness/Aid)
bite off more than one can chew   try to do more than one can (Limitations)
blow up   explode with anger or strong feeling; lose control of oneself (Control of Anger)
brainstorm   confer with another to solve a problem (Cooperation)
breathe down one's neck   stand very near and watch someone very closely (Privacy)
breathing space   enough room (Privacy)
bring up the rear   do least well; do the most poorly of a group; be last (Individual Achievement)
burn oneself out   wear oneself out by using all of one's energy or strength (Limitations)
burn the midnight oil   study very late at night (Hard Work)
bury the hatchet   settle a quarrel; make peace (Harmony)
button one's lips   stop talking; keep a secret; be quiet (Harmony)

cannot change a leopard's spots   recognize that a person will not or cannot change (Improbability of Desired Outcome)
cards stacked against one   an unfair disadvantage (Improbability of Desired Outcome)
come apart at the seams   become upset to the point where one loses self-control and composure as if having suffered a nervous breakdown (Control of Emotions)
count to ten   count from one to ten to have enough time to calm down or regain control; postpone action when angry (Control of Anger)
crash a party   attend a social function without an invitation (Privacy)
cut someone to the quick   hurt someone's feelings deeply (Kindness/Aid)
cut the apron strings   sever a dependency from one's mother (Independence)

do back-breaking work   do very difficult physical work (Hard Work)
do the footwork   carry out another's plan, especially by attending to the details (Kindness/Aid)
drag one's feet   act slowly or reluctantly (Speed/Efficiency)
drink like a fish   consume alcoholic drinks excessively (Limitations)
duck the issue   avoid an unpleasant job (Responsibility)

eat like a horse   eat excessively (Limitations)
elbow one's way in   force oneself upon others (Privacy)
elbow room   enough room to move around comfortably (Privacy)
eyes are bigger than one's stomach   think one can eat more than one is able (Limitations)

face up to something   accept something unpleasant (Responsibility)
fair shake   honest treatment (Fair Play)
fall apart   lose control of oneself (Control of Emotions)
fall down on the job   fail to work well (Hard Work)
feather in one's cap   something to be proud of; an honor (Individual Achievement)
feel blue   be sad (Happiness)
feel fenced in   feel kept from doing what one would like (Privacy)
feel hemmed in   feel kept from doing what one would like (Privacy)
feel like a million bucks   be in a very good mood (Happiness)
find middle ground   find a place halfway between the two sides of an argument (Compromise)
flip out   go insane; become crazy (Control of Emotions)
flow with the tide   accept what goes on; not object (Harmony)
fly off the handle   become very angry (Control of Anger)

get ahead become successful (Individual Achievement)

get away with murder do something very bad without being punished (Fair Play)

get burned be severely wronged (Fair Play)

get down to the nuts and bolts get started on the most important thing to talk about or know (Problem-Solving Ability)

get moving get started (Speed/Efficiency)

get off someone's back stop bothering or criticizing someone (Harmony)

get one's feet wet begin; do something for the first time (Experience)

get something off one's chest unload a burden (Honesty/Directness)

get the ball rolling start an activity or action; make a beginning (Speed/Efficiency)

get the show on the road start an activity (Speed/Efficiency)

get to the heart of something find and go to the most important part of something (Problem-Solving Ability)

get up on the wrong side of the bed awake in a bad mood (Friendliness)

give someone a piece of one's mind scold angrily; say what one really thinks in an angry way (Control of Anger)

give someone the ax abruptly finish a relationship; fire an employee without warning (Fair Play)

give someone the cold shoulder treat someone in an unfriendly way (Friendliness)

give someone the shirt off one's back be very generous (Kindness/Aid)

give up stop trying; surrender (Perseverance)

give-and-take giving up by people on different sides a part of what one wants so that they can agree (Compromise)

go halfway sacrifice part of what one wants to reach an agreement with someone (Compromise)

go it alone do something by oneself with no help (Cooperation)

go out of one's way for someone make an extra effort; do more than usual (Kindness/Aid)

go through with something finish; do as planned or agreed (Perseverance)

go to bat for someone help someone in trouble or need (Kindness/Aid)

go to one's head think that one is too important (Humility)

go to pieces lose emotional self-control (Control of Emotions)

go to the school of hard knocks learn from work and troubles and not from formal education (Experience)

goof off not work seriously (Hard Work)

grit one's teeth refrain from showing anger outwardly (Control of Anger)

hand is dealt out of one's control or responsibility (Improbability of Desired Outcome)

handle someone with kid gloves treat very gently and carefully (Harmony)

hang in there continue doing; not quit (Perseverance)

have a bone to pick with someone have a reason for dispute; have something to complain or argue about (Friendliness)

have a golden touch make money easily (Ease of Effort)

have a green thumb have a talent for gardening; have an ability to make things grow (Ease of Effort)

have a head on one's shoulders be smart (Thinking Ability)

have a heart be kind, generous, or sympathetic (Kindness/Aid)

have a heart of gold have a kind, generous, or forgiving nature (Kindness/Aid)

have a heart of stone have no pity (Kindness/Aid)

have a knack for something be able to do something easily (Ease of Effort)

have a lot on the ball be smart (Thinking Ability)

have a mind of one's own be an independent thinker (Independence)

have a nose for something have the ability to sense or discover as if by smell (Ease of Effort)

have a screw loose act in a strange way; be foolish (Thinking Ability)

have a snowball's chance in hell have no chance at all (Improbability of Desired Outcome)

have a sunny disposition always be pleasant and cheerful (Friendliness)

have a swollen head exaggerate one's importance (Humility)

have lead in one's feet   be slow in walking or moving (Speed/Efficiency)
have two left feet   walk awkwardly (Ease of Effort)
heart goes out to someone   feel very sorry for; feel pity for (Kindness/Aid)
heart is in the right place   have good intentions (Kindness/Aid)
hem and haw   avoid giving a clear answer (Problem-Solving Ability)
hit the books   study in a serious way (Hard Work)
hit the bull's eye   go to the main part of a matter (Problem-Solving Ability)
hit the nail on the head   get something exactly right (Problem-Solving Ability)
hold one's head up   show self-respect; not be ashamed; be brave (Control of Emotions)
hold one's temper   not become angry (Control of Anger)
hold one's tongue   be silent; not talk (Harmony)

icy stare   very unfriendly look (Friendliness)
in a flash   very suddenly; very quickly (Speed/Efficiency)
in no time   in very little time (Speed/Efficiency)
in nothing flat   in very little time (Speed/Efficiency)
iron things out   reach an agreement about a difference (Harmony)

join forces   unite one's strengths with others (Cooperation)
jump down someone's throat   suddenly become very angry at someone (Harmony)

keep a civil tongue   be polite in speaking, although angry (Control of Anger)
keep a stiff upper lip   be brave; face trouble bravely (Control of Emotions)
keep one's chin up   be brave; face trouble with courage (Control of Emotions)
keep one's nose to the grindstone   work hard all of the time (Hard Work)
keep someone at arm's length   avoid someone's company (Privacy)
kick up a fuss   make trouble; make a disturbance (Harmony)
know something like the back of one's hand   know thoroughly and completely (Experience)
know the ropes   have a special knowledge of a job; know how to do something (Experience)

lay one's cards on the table   tell all; be completely open (Honesty/Directness)
lead someone by the nose   have full control of someone (Independence)
leave a bad taste in one's mouth   leave a bad impression (Friendliness)
leave someone high and dry   leave without anyone to help (Responsibility)
lend a hand   help someone (Cooperation)
lend someone an ear   listen to (Kindness/Aid)
let off steam   decrease strong feeling, often anger, through activity or talking (Control of Anger)
let sleeping dogs lie   not anger or cause trouble if not necessary (Harmony)
let well enough alone   be satisfied with what is good enough; not try to improve something because that might make things worse (Harmony)
like a bat out of hell   extremely quickly (Speed/Efficiency)
live and learn   learn more as life goes on; learn by experience (Experience)
look like one has the weight of the world on one's shoulders   be very tired and worried (Happiness)
look like one lost one's best friend   look very unhappy (Happiness)
look someone in the eye   meet or face directly (Honesty/Directness)
lose one's head   lose control of oneself; become upset (Limitations)

make a pig out of oneself   eat in excess (Limitations)
make someone's blood boil   make someone very angry (Control of Anger)
make waves   create a disturbance (Harmony)
meet someone halfway   give up part of what you want to reach an agreement with someone (Compromise)
middle-of-the-road   halfway between two opposite sides (Compromise)
mind one's own business   not interfere with what someone else is doing (Harmony)
miss the mark   not understand the most important thing (Problem-Solving Ability)
move in on someone   take over something that belongs to another (Privacy)

not bat an eyelash not show surprise, fear, or interest; not show what one is feeling (Control of Emotions)

not be born yesterday not be inexperienced and easily fooled (Experience)

not have anything between the ears be stupid (Thinking Ability)

not hold a candle to not be fit to be compared with; not be in the same class with (Individual Achievement)

not know enough to come in out of the rain not have good sense; not know how to take care of oneself (Thinking Ability)

not know whether one is coming or going not be able to think clearly; not know what to do (Thinking Ability)

open a can of worms raise a complex problem or complicated situation (Harmony)

pass the buck shift or escape responsibility or blame; put the duty or blame on someone else (Responsiblity)

pick someone's brain ask someone a lot of questions in order to get information (Thinking Ability)

pitch in help someone

play second fiddle to someone act a smaller part; be less noticed (Individual Achievement)

play with half a deck be stupid; retarded (Thinking Ability)

point one's finger at someone accuse someone else (Responsibility)

pool one's resources combine one's strengths with another (Cooperation)

pull oneself together become calm after being excited; recover self-control (Control of Emotions)

pull the wool over someone's eyes deceive someone (Honesty/Directness)

put heads together consult with one another to work out problems (Cooperation)

put on airs exaggerate one's importance (Humility)

put on one's thinking cap think long and hard about a problem (Thinking Ability)

put someone in someone's place reduce someone's pride (Humility)

quick as a wink in very little time (Speed/Efficiency)

rake someone over the coals criticize sharply (Fair Play)

reach the boiling point become very angry (Control of Anger)

rock the boat make trouble and risk losing or upsetting something (Harmony)

roll up one's sleeves get ready for a hard job; prepare to work hard or seriously (Speed/Efficiency)

run around like a chicken with its head cut off by very active or busy, but with no direction or organization (Speed/Efficiency)

run oneself ragged make oneself excessively tired by trying to do too much work (Limitations)

scrape the bottom of the barrel use or take whatever is left after the best has been taken (Individual Achievement)

see eye to eye agree fully; hold exactly the same opinion (Harmony)

see red become very angry (Control of Anger)

see the writing on the wall realize that something will happen (Improbability of Desired Outcome)

shake a leg go fast; hurry (Speed/Efficiency)

shoulder the responsibility be responsible for (Responsibility)

show off try to attract attention (Humility)

sit up and take notice be surprised into noticing something (Individual Achievement)

skirt the issue avoid taking a position (Problem-Solving Ability)

spread oneself too thin become involved in too many activities (Limitations)

stand on one's own two feet depend on oneself (Independence)

steal the show act or do so well that one gets most of the attention (Individual Achievement)

stick to one's guns hold onto an opinion in spite of pressure to change it (Compromise)

stick with something continue doing; not quit (Perseverance)

strike off on one's own   do something alone (Cooperation)

strut like a rooster   walk in a very proud way (Humility)

sweat something out   wait anxiously; worry while waiting (Perseverance)

tailgate   drive too closely behind another car (Privacy)

take it easy   avoid hard work; relax (Limitation)

take one's hat off to someone   give honor, praise, and respect to (Individual Achievement)

take someone down a notch or two   humble a person (Humility)

take the bull by the horns   take definite action and not care about risks (Problem-Solving Ability)

talk behind someone's back   gossip about someone without that person's knowledge (Honesty/Directness)

talk until one is blue in the face   talk excessively but not convincingly (Honesty/Directness)

tell it like it is   tell the truth (Honesty/Directness)

think one is God's gift to mankind   think extremely highly of oneself (Humility)

throw a monkey wrench into something   cause something that is going smoothly to stop (Harmony)

throw someone a curve   mislead or deceive someone; surprise someone in an unpleasant way (Fair Play)

tie one's hands   make someone unable to do something (usually used in the passive) (Improbability of Desired Outcome)

toot one's own horn   congratulate oneself publicly on one's achievements (Humility)

turn one's back on someone   turn and look away from someone (Friendliness)

turn one's nose up at someone   act as though someone is not good enough (Friendliness)

two heads are better than one   two people working together can achieve more than one person (Cooperation)

upset the applecart   change something, often by surprise or accident (Harmony)

walk on air   feel happy and excited (Happiness)

welcome someone with open arms   greet with words or actions showing that one is glad to see another (Friendliness)

whip the pants off someone   win by a wide margin (Individual Achievement)

work like a dog   work hard and seriously (Hard Work)

work one's fingers to the bone   work very hard (Hard Work)

worm out of something   avoid responsibility (Responsibility)

zero in on something   discard irrelevant material and get to the main issue (Problem-Solving Ability)